ALSO BY AMERICA'S TEST KITCHEN

For a Full Listing of All Our Books

CooksIllustrated.com

AmericasTestKitchen.com

PRAISE FOR AMERICA'S TEST KITCHEN TITLES

"The book's depth, breadth, and practicality makes it a must-have for seafood lovers."

PUBLISHERS WEEKLY (STARRED REVIEW) ON *FOOLPROOF FISH*

"Another flawless entry in the America's Test Kitchen canon, *Bowls* guides readers of all culinary skill levels in composing one-bowl meals from a variety of cuisines."

BUZZFEED BOOKS ON *BOWLS*

Selected as the Cookbook Award Winner of 2019 in the Health and Special Diet Category

INTERNATIONAL ASSOCIATION OF CULINARY PROFESSIONALS (IACP) ON *THE COMPLETE DIABETES COOKBOOK*

"Diabetics and all health-conscious home cooks will find great information on almost every page."

BOOKLIST (STARRED REVIEW) ON *THE COMPLETE DIABETES COOKBOOK*

"This is a wonderful, useful guide to healthy eating."

PUBLISHERS WEEKLY ON *NUTRITIOUS DELICIOUS*

"*The Perfect Cookie*. . . is, in a word, perfect. This is an important and substantial cookbook. . . . If you love cookies, but have been a tad shy to bake on your own, all your fears will be dissipated. This is one book you can use for years with magnificently happy results."

THE HUFFINGTON POST ON *THE PERFECT COOKIE*

Selected as one of the 10 Best New Cookbooks of 2017

THE LA TIMES ON *THE PERFECT COOKIE*

"The sum total of exhaustive experimentation . . . anyone interested in gluten-free cookery simply shouldn't be without it."

NIGELLA LAWSON ON *THE HOW CAN IT BE GLUTEN-FREE COOKBOOK*

"True to its name, this smart and endlessly enlightening cookbook is about as definitive as it's possible to get in the modern vegetarian realm."

MEN'S JOURNAL ON *THE COMPLETE VEGETARIAN COOKBOOK*

"If you're a home cook who loves long introductions that tell you why a dish works followed by lots of step-by-step hand holding, then you'll love *Vegetables Illustrated*."

THE WALL STREET JOURNAL ON *VEGETABLES ILLUSTRATED*

"A one-volume kitchen seminar, addressing in one smart chapter after another the sometimes surprising whys behind a cook's best practices. . . . You get the myth, the theory, the science, and the proof, all rigorously interrogated as only America's Test Kitchen can do."

NPR ON *THE SCIENCE OF GOOD COOKING*

"The 21st-century *Fannie Farmer Cookbook* or *The Joy of Cooking*. If you had to have one cookbook and that's all you could have, this one would do it."

CBS SAN FRANCISCO ON *THE NEW FAMILY COOKBOOK*

"Some 2,500 photos walk readers through 600 painstakingly tested recipes, leaving little room for error."

ASSOCIATED PRESS ON *THE AMERICA'S TEST KITCHEN COOKING SCHOOL COOKBOOK*

"The go-to gift book for newlyweds, small families, or empty nesters."

ORLANDO SENTINEL ON *THE COMPLETE COOKING FOR TWO COOKBOOK*

"Some books impress by the sheer audacity of their ambition. Backed by the magazine's famed mission to test every recipe relentlessly until it is the best it can be, this nearly 900-page volume lands with an authoritative wallop."

CHICAGO TRIBUNE ON *THE COOK'S ILLUSTRATED COOKBOOK*

"This impressive installment from America's Test Kitchen equips readers with dozens of repertoire-worthy recipes. . . . This is a must-have for beginner cooks and more experienced ones who wish to sharpen their skills."

PUBLISHERS WEEKLY (STARRED REVIEW) ON *THE NEW ESSENTIALS COOKBOOK*

FIVE
ingredient
DINNERS

100+ FAST, FLAVORFUL MEALS

AMERICA'S TEST KITCHEN

Library of Congress Cataloging-in-Publication Data

Names: America's Test Kitchen (Firm), author.
Title: Five-ingredient dinners : 100+ fast, flavorful
    meals / America's Test Kitchen.
Description: Boston, MA : America's Test Kitchen,
    [2021] | Includes index.
Identifiers: LCCN 2021021478 (print) | LCCN
    2021021479 (ebook) | ISBN 9781948703925 |
    ISBN 9781948703932 (ebook)
Subjects: LCSH: Quick and easy cooking. | LCGFT:
    Cookbooks.
Classification: LCC TX833.5 .A4455 2021 (print) |
    LCC TX833.5 (ebook) | DDC 641.5/12--dc23
LC record available at https://lccn.loc.
    gov/2021021478
LC ebook record available at https://lccn.loc.
    gov/2021021479

AMERICA'S TEST KITCHEN
21 Drydock Avenue, Boston, MA 02210

Printed in Canada
10 9 8 7 6 5 4 3 2 1

Distributed by Penguin Random House
Publisher Services
Tel: 800.733.3000

Pictured on front cover Cumin-Spiced Chicken
Thighs with Cauliflower Couscous (page 43)

Pictured on back cover (clockwise from top left)
Sweet Potato, Celery Root, and Apple Hash with
Sausage and Eggs (page 89), Cauliflower Pasta with
Browned Butter–Sage Sauce (page 150), Grilled
Garam Masala Chicken, Tomatoes, and Naan
with Chutney (page 211), Salmon and Rice with
Cucumber Salad (page 103), Potato and Onion
Pizza with Rosemary and Goat Cheese (page 191),
and Lamb Meatballs with Pearl Couscous (page 143)

Editorial Director, Books **Adam Kowit**
Executive Food Editor **Dan Zuccarello**
Deputy Food Editor **Stephanie Pixley**
Executive Managing Editor **Debra Hudak**
Senior Editors **Camila Chaparro, Leah Colins,
    Sara Mayer, and Russell Selander**
Associate Editors **Sam Block and Brenna Donovan**
Test Cook **Carmen Dongo**
Additional Recipe Development **Anne Wolf**
Assistant Editors **Emily Rahravan and
    Sara Zatopek**
Design Director **Lindsey Timko Chandler**
Deputy Art Director **Katie Barranger**
Graphic Designer **Molly Gillespie**
Photography Director **Julie Bozzo Cote**
Photography Producer **Meredith Mulcahy**
Senior Staff Photographers **Steve Klise and
    Daniel J. van Ackere**
Staff Photographer **Kevin White**
Additional Photography **Nina Gallant,
    Joseph Keller, and Carl Tremblay**
Food Styling **Joy Howard, Catrine Kelty,
    Steve Klise, Chantal Lambeth, Ashley Moore,
    Christie Morrison, Marie Piraino,
    Elle Simone Scott, and Kendra Smith**
Photoshoot Kitchen Team
    Photo Team and Special Events Manager
    Alli Berkey
    Lead Test Cook **Eric Haessler**
    Test Cooks **Hannah Fenton,
    Jacqueline Gochenouer, and
    Gina McCreadie**
    Assistant Test Cooks **Kristen Bango,
    Hisham Hassan, and Christa West**
Illustration **Erin Griffiths**
Senior Manager, Publishing Operations
    Taylor Argenzio
Imaging Manager **Lauren Robbins**
Production and Imaging Specialists
    **Tricia Neumyer, Dennis Noble,
    and Amanda Yong**
Copy Editor **Deri Reed**
Proofreader **Kelly Gauthier**
Indexer **Elizabeth Parson**

Chief Creative Officer **Jack Bishop**
Executive Editorial Directors **Julia Collin Davison
    and Bridget Lancaster**

Contents

Welcome to America's Test Kitchen

This book has been tested, written, and edited by the folks at America's Test Kitchen, where curious cooks become confident cooks. Located in Boston's Seaport District in the historic Innovation and Design Building, it features 15,000 square feet of kitchen space including multiple photography and video studios. It is the home of *Cook's Illustrated* magazine and *Cook's Country* magazine and is the workday destination for more than 60 test cooks, editors, and cookware specialists. Our mission is to empower and inspire confidence, community, and creativity in the kitchen.

We start the process of testing a recipe with a complete lack of preconceptions, which means that we accept no claim, no technique, and no recipe at face value. We simply assemble as many variations as possible, test a half-dozen of the most promising, and taste the results blind. We then construct our own recipe and continue to test it, varying ingredients, techniques, and cooking times until we reach a consensus. As we like to say in the test kitchen, "We make the mistakes so you don't have to." The result, we hope, is the best version of a particular recipe, but we realize that only you can be the final judge of our success (or failure). We use the same rigorous approach when we test equipment and taste ingredients.

All of this would not be possible without a belief that good cooking, much like good music, is based on a foundation of objective technique. Some people like spicy foods and others don't, but there is a right way to sauté, there is a best way to cook a pot roast, and there are measurable scientific principles involved in producing perfectly beaten, stable egg whites. Our ultimate goal is to investigate the fundamental principles of cooking to give you the techniques, tools, and ingredients you need to become a better cook. It is as simple as that.

To see what goes on behind the scenes at America's Test Kitchen, check out our social media channels for kitchen snapshots, exclusive content, video tips, and much more. You can watch us work (in our actual test kitchen) by tuning in to *America's Test Kitchen* or *Cook's Country* on public television or on our websites. Listen to *Proof*, *Mystery Recipe*, and *The Walk-In* (AmericasTestKitchen.com/podcasts) to hear engaging, complex stories about people and food. Want to hone your cooking skills or finally learn how to bake—with an America's Test Kitchen test cook? Enroll in one of our online cooking classes. And you can engage the next generation of home cooks with kid-tested recipes from America's Test Kitchen Kids.

Our community of home recipe testers provides valuable feedback on recipes under development by ensuring that they are foolproof. You can help us investigate the how and why behind successful recipes from your home kitchen. (Sign up at AmericasTestKitchen.com/recipe_testing.)

However you choose to visit us, we welcome you into our kitchen, where you can stand by our side as we test our way to the best recipes in America.

facebook.com/AmericasTestKitchen
twitter.com/TestKitchen
youtube.com/AmericasTestKitchen
instagram.com/TestKitchen
pinterest.com/TestKitchen

AmericasTestKitchen.com
CooksIllustrated.com
CooksCountry.com
OnlineCookingSchool.com
AmericasTestKitchen.com/kids

Dinner
in Five

This is a cookbook for your real life. The days when you're busy, exhausted, or just don't feel like spending a lot of time and energy cooking (we've all been there!). You want a delicious meal without the hassle of a lengthy ingredient list and time-consuming cooking process, and you're looking to cut corners without sacrificing quality. Tonight's not the night for a multi-course meal, you need something a bit more manageable. But that doesn't mean you shouldn't have something absolutely scrumptious.

With recipes for back-pocket dinners using just five ingredients that require little in the way of planning, you've come to the right place.

To create meals that are short on ingredients but not on flavor, we followed three guidelines. We used test cook–approved (but totally achievable) cooking techniques to transform ingredients into something really special. We made our ingredients work overtime by using every last part (even ones we might usually toss). And we relied on store-bought items that squeeze multiple flavors into one jar (think: pesto or tomatillo salsa); pack a punch (like gochujang); or make our lives just a little bit easier (hello, pizza dough).

And when we say five ingredients, we mean it. The only exceptions (what we call our "staples") are salt, pepper, and oil or butter. On every page, the staple ingredients are separated from the other main ingredients so you can see what you need at a glance.

With each recipe, a test cook or editor's commentary gives an inside peek into the recipe creation process and helps inspire you with tales from our home kitchens—because, yes, these are the recipes we turn to again and again when we're feeling a little frazzled.

What these recipes lack in ingredients, they more than make up for in flavor and creativity. So put down the takeout menu and back away from the frozen dinner aisle, we're here to save the day.

Meet the Team

Get acquainted with the team of test cooks and editors who put this book together.

SAM BLOCK

After culinary school, I worked in restaurants in my home state of New Jersey before jumping at the opportunity to travel the world performing culinary demonstrations on cruise ships as an ATK host. Now I'm back stateside developing recipes to inspire home cook creativity.

My favorite time-saving tip: I always keep a "garbage bowl" (just a large mixing bowl) nearby to corral all of my scraps.

My favorite kitchen tool: A bench scraper helps me scoop up food more efficiently (and is much safer than a knife).

CARMEN DONGO

I cooked on many a stovetop throughout Boston and beyond, realizing along the way that taking strides towards increasing food access was my true calling. I believe eating well is an act of radical self care, and my goal is to empower cooks (and would-be cooks) everywhere to take that step.

My favorite time-saving tip: Mindfulness! I read through the recipe and visualize each step before I even start to cook.

My favorite kitchen tool: Eco-friendly sponge cloths as an alternative to single-use paper towels. They can tackle any spill and they last for months.

BRENNA DONOVAN

I grew up in upstate New York surrounded by local farm stands (and a whole lot of cows)—it's where my appreciation for seasonal, delicious food began. Now, I'm an avid home cook and cookbook editor who puts flaky salt on everything and is always in the mood for breakfast—no matter the time of day.

My favorite time-saving tip: Flex your multitasking skills. Roasting veggies or waiting for rice to cook? Use that time to prep other ingredients or get a head start on dishes (ugh).

My favorite kitchen tool: A mini whisk is the perfect size for any task, is easy to clean, and hardly takes up any drawer space.

CAMILA CHAPARRO

I traded in a PhD and a career in international nutrition research for culinary school and recipe development. As a mom of two, I consider a recipe a true success when everyone at the table will eat it and believe that if there's a vegetable you don't like, you just haven't found the right way to cook it yet.

My favorite time-saving tip: I like to keep a tray of essentials (like a cruet of oil and a bowl of salt) at the ready.

My favorite kitchen tool: A large cutting board means nothing falls off, whether I'm chopping lots of vegetables or breaking down a chicken.

LEAH COLINS

I spent a few years cheffing it in restaurants from coast to coast. These days I love growing roses, spicy peppers, sweet little babies, and creating simple dinners and delicious breads at home (not necessarily in that order!).

My favorite time-saving tip: I try to clean as I cook! That way I can savor my meal without dreading cleanup.

My favorite kitchen tool: A digital timer helps me keep track of multiple dishes at once and is easy to bring with me when I'm chasing after my toddler.

STEPHANIE PIXLEY

When I was a kid, I ate dinner with my family at the dining room table every night of the week. While dinners are usually more casual for me now, I still love the ritual of cooking and presenting a meal to my family, though I still try to wriggle out of cleanup.

My favorite time-saving tip: I always prep ingredients ahead of time; it makes following the recipe so much easier!

My favorite kitchen tool: I love instant-read thermometers because they take the guesswork out of cooking.

RUSSELL SELANDER

After a short stint in an office job post-graduation, I enrolled in culinary school and never looked back. Now, as a father of three, I'm always trying to strike a balance between from-scratch cooking and store-bought substitutes.

My favorite time-saving tip: Frozen vegetables can get a bad rap, but I love them—especially as a low-effort way to sneak veggies into homemade mac and cheese for my kids.

My favorite kitchen tool: Touchless tools, like an automatic soap dispenser, so I don't have to touch anything with raw-chicken-covered hands.

Turn to Technique

To harness big flavors with a small ingredient list, we relied on simple techniques to coax the maximum amount of *oomph* out of each component. Because it's not just about the ingredients you use, but what you do to them.

BECOME FOND OF FOND

The browned bits that stick to the bottom of the pan when you sear meat are called fond—and they are a gold mine of savory flavor. Cooking bacon or crispy-skinned chicken thighs? Take advantage of the fond-studded leftover fat in the pan to sauté your vegetables or toast your grains. We also use fond to create a quick broth by deglazing the hot pan with liquid (plain old water works just fine) and scraping the fond free with a wooden spoon. We've used this trick to create a beefy ramen broth after cooking steak tips (page 57) and a rich chicken broth to hydrate bulgur (page 33).

DON'T BE SALTY (or, do)

Salt is the not-so-secret ingredient that brings excellence to eggs, turns pasta from drab to delicious, and makes your tomatoes taste tomatoier. If your meal's feeling a little "meh," salt can be the answer. But you shouldn't wait until the dish is almost on the table to shake on some of the good stuff. Adding small amounts of salt throughout the cooking process (instead of only at the end) gives it time to migrate into the pieces of food, seasoning them from within. That "season to taste" directive is there for a reason, though. It not only helps you adjust to your own salty preferences, but also—because slight variations in ingredients and cooking times affect the saltiness of a dish—it helps prevent oversalting. And because temperature impacts our perception of saltiness, a good rule of thumb is to taste the dish at serving temperature and adjust the salt accordingly.

The Bitter End

Salt does so much more than just make things taste salty—it actually makes food taste more like itself. How? By masking bitterness. Because our taste buds have many more receptors for bitterness than for the other four basic tastes (sweet, sour, salty, and umami), bitterness can often overwhelm other flavors present in food. Salt works to block the taste of bitter compounds, thereby enhancing other, less prominent flavors. We've even been known to sprinkle a little salt into a full pot of coffee to temper coffee's signature bite.

USE SMOKE AS AN INGREDIENT (yes, really)

Grilling not only satisfies our most primal urges (fire good) but it also imparts a smoky flavor that just can't be replicated indoors. As a result, you don't need as many sauces and spices to gussy up an otherwise simple meal—the grill is really an ingredient itself, bringing smokiness, caramelization, and char to anything on it. It's no wonder we devoted an entire chapter to it. The true magic happens when rendered fat from a steak or piece of chicken drips down through the grates and evaporates, infusing that piece of protein with even more aromatic deliciousness. But it's not just meat that benefits from the flame—the sugars found in vegetables (and fruit!) are intensified when caramelized, which pairs perfectly with the hint of smoke the grill leaves behind.

LET IT BLOOM

Many spices and spice blends will taste fuller and more complex (and less flat and dusty) if they are "bloomed," or briefly cooked in butter or oil. Blooming spices doesn't have to be complicated—it's as simple as heating the spices in fat a few seconds ahead of the other ingredients in your dish. Blooming draws out maximum spice flavor without really adding an extra step—you'd need to add the spices to the dish at some point anyway. And while heat unlocks the door, it's important to make sure the fat isn't too hot as it can scorch the spices.

WHEN IN DOUBT, ADD A DRIZZLE

It's remarkable what a simple drizzle of extra-virgin olive oil just before serving can do. Like a squeeze of lemon or sprinkle of flaky salt, EVOO is the perfect last-minute, restaurant-worthy move that wakes up the flavors of your dish, bringing a rich, fruity flavor and gorgeous ready-for-its-closeup shine. And because oil is one of our staples, it's like a simple sauce without any added ingredients.

Turn to Technique

BUTTER ME UP

Whether it's in a sauce or slathered on toast, everything is better with butter. But to really take butter to the next level, make a compound butter or browned butter. Dollop garlic compound butter over grilled strip steaks (page 223), toss orange-tarragon butter with just-crunchy-enough sautéed green beans (page 109), or make a honey-cinnamon butter to spread on any baked good you can get your hands on. And infuse that browned butter with sage and turn it into a glossy sauce to coat cauliflower pasta (page 150), or spoon it over fish or even vanilla ice cream.

Last-Minute Softened Butter

There's nothing worse than starting a recipe that calls for softened butter only to realize you forgot to take it out of the fridge in time. Never fear: Here are two tried-and-true ways to get spreadable, stat.

Counter method: Cut butter into small pieces (to create more surface area). Place butter on plate and wait about 30 minutes. Once butter gives to light pressure (try to push your fingertip into it), it's ready to use.

Microwave method: Cut butter into small pieces and place on microwave-safe plate. Heat in microwave at 50 percent power for 5 to 10 seconds. Check butter with fingertip test. Heat for another 5 to 10 seconds if necessary.

Here's some inspiration for the Make-It-Your-Way Compound Butter to get you started:

- Thai red curry paste + cilantro
- Anchovies + shallots
- Capers + dill
- White miso + scallions
- Feta + mint
- Garlic + parsley
- Lemon zest + chives
- Blue cheese + thyme
- Whole-grain mustard + honey
- Lime zest + ginger
- Hoisin sauce + serrano chile
- Orange zest + tarragon

Make-It-Your-Way Compound Butter

MAKES: 4 TABLESPOONS

Stirring seasonings into softened butter is an easy way to make a rich, flavor-packed condiment to melt over a finished dish, turning it into a luxurious sauce. And because butter is one of our staple ingredients, you can mix it together with ingredients already being used in the recipe (like shallots, garlic, citrus zest, or herbs) for an extra hit of flavor with nary an extra ingredient.

Make it: Soften 4 tablespoons unsalted butter and mix in ¼ teaspoon to 3 tablespoons of whatever ingredients you're already using in your recipe. (The amount will depend on the ingredient, use less for potent spices like cayenne but more for milder add-ins like fresh herbs.) Dollop over the finished dish.

Store it: Wrap the compound butter in plastic wrap and roll it into a log. Keep it in the refrigerator for up to 4 days or freeze it for up to 2 months.

TIPS

Mince, don't chop: For everything to incorporate evenly, make sure to mince each component—you want the flavors to disperse evenly throughout the butter, and nothing kills a good bite like an unexpected oversize chunk of garlic.

Unsalted butter is best: To have final control over the seasoning level of your compound butter, stick with unsalted butter for a blank slate—you can always add salt if you think it needs it. You might even want to skip the extra seasoning altogether if you're working with saltier ingredients (like miso).

Make sure the butter is room temp: A straight-from-the-refrigerator stick of butter typically takes about 2 hours on the counter to reach room temperature (see "Last-Minute Softened Butter," opposite, for tips on shortening that 2-hour time frame). It should give slightly when pressed. Because the butter will warm up as you mix it with stir-ins, make sure you don't go much beyond that.

Browned Butter

MAKES: 4 TABLESPOONS

Browned butter is the toasty, nutty addition your warm and cozy meals have been craving. Made from taking butter past the point of melted and cooking it until its milk solids deepen to a dark golden brown, this one-ingredient sauce is the perfect companion to sweet and savory eats alike.

Make it: Heat 4 tablespoons unsalted butter in a medium skillet over medium-high heat until melted, about 2 minutes, stirring or swirling the skillet constantly. Almost immediately, you'll see tiny specks settling to the bottom of the pan—these are the milk solids that give the browned butter its characteristic color and flavor. Continue to cook, swirling the skillet and stirring constantly with a rubber spatula, until the butter is dark golden brown and has a nutty aroma, 1 to 3 minutes longer. As soon as the butter turns chestnut brown and smells toasty, remove the pan from the heat. Use browned butter immediately or transfer it to another container. Otherwise, the residual heat from the hot pan may burn it.

TIPS

Use the right skillet: Don't be tempted to use a dark skillet such as most nonstick skillets. You need a stainless-steel or enameled cast-iron skillet to easily monitor the color of the butter.

Use the right butter: Use only unsalted butter. Salted butter foams more when melted than unsalted does, which can make it difficult to monitor the color.

Scrape out the pan: Much of the flavor of browned butter is in the browned milk solids. Make sure you get every last bit out of the pan.

Make Ingredients Work Overtime

(and cut down on food waste while you're at it)

By making ingredients pull double-duty, you'll think twice before tossing something in the trash or down the drain. We've got creative ideas for stretching your ingredients a little further (like turning usually-discarded elements into a garnish or flavor-booster), and helping minimize your food waste.

Sautéed Cod with Roasted Cauliflower and Radishes, page 112

← ROOT VEGETABLES

Root vegetables like carrots, beets, and radishes are often sold with their greens still attached. Use the feathery carrot tops like an herb: Finely chop to use as a garnish or blend into pesto with an equal amount of basil. And double up on your veggie intake by sautéing or braising beet or radish greens as you would Swiss chard or kale. We also like finely chopping radish tops to use as a garnish in lieu of herbs.

Tip: Remove the greens from the vegetables when you get home from the grocery store and store them separately—they'll take up less space in your fridge, and it makes it much easier to sort through the greens to get rid of any funky-looking ones.

Grilled Chicken, Asparagus, and Endive with Gremolata, page 209

← CITRUS

We all know that a final spritz of lemon (or lime) juice brightens up a finished dish, but citrus is good for more than just a squeeze—the zest (colored part of the peel) has concentrated, aromatic oils that bring a potent zing (without the tartness) to your recipes. Before cutting into the citrus, remove the zest with a Microplane and stir it into a pan sauce, toss it with crispy bread crumbs, or whip up a quick gremolata.

Tip: Get in the habit of always zesting your citrus before you cut into it, even if you don't plan on using it right away—just separate the grated zest into ½- or 1-teaspoon piles on a plate and freeze. Once the piles are frozen, store them in a zipper-lock freezer bag. Just need the zest? Wrap the zested fruit in plastic before refrigerating it to keep it fresh for when you're ready to juice.

PICKLE-Y THINGS →

Instead of tossing out a jar of pickle juice after finishing the last spear, save that brine for anything that needs a little perking up. But the fun doesn't stop with pickles: Whisk giardiniera liquid into a vinaigrette, add pickled jalapeño brine to coleslaw, or slip some pepperoncini juice into a Bloody Mary. Just remember, the vinegar in pickle brine is slightly diluted by water pulled from the vegetables, so don't substitute it one-for-one for vinegar or lemon juice.

Tip: Make your own pickled onions by adding thinly sliced onions to the leftover brine in a jar of pickles (or even pickled peppers) and let them marinate in the refrigerator for a few days. Drain 'em and use as a topping for tacos or sandwiches or in salads.

Chicken Salad with Whole-Grain
Mustard Vinaigrette, page 25

MARINATED THINGS →

If you've got a penchant for hoarding jars of fancy-seeming flavor-packed goodies like marinated feta or sun-dried tomatoes in oil, you're not alone. It's one of our favorite ways to add a massive hit of flavor with just one ingredient. But we also love using the oft-forgotten flavorful oil itself as a way to jazz things up. You can find us using the oil in vinaigrettes and sauces, drizzling it over warm beans with a runny egg, and even dipping crusty bread into it as a pre-dinner snack.

Tip: When you've used all of the sun-dried tomatoes in the jar, add some vinegar and shake it up to make a quick, in-the-jar salad dressing.

Shrimp with Warm Barley Salad, page 122

CANNED BEANS →

Your first instinct when opening a can of beans might be to drain and rinse, but that starchy liquid is worth keeping around. It adds flavor and body to a finished dish, bringing a creaminess that's something like what you get when you toss pasta with its own cooking water. Just one word of caution: Depending on the brand, the liquid can often be salty, so adjust seasoning as needed.

Tip: Too much bean-can liquid for what you're cooking? Don't get rid of the extra. Instead, freeze it in 1-tablespoon portions in ice cube trays. Once the bean liquid is frozen solid, transfer the cubes to a freezer bag for future use. (Or, just keep the liquid in a container in the fridge if you plan to use it within a week.)

'Nduja with Beans and Greens, page 90

Kimchi and Ham Steak Fried Rice, page 93

← SCALLIONS

If there were an award for "Most Likely to Be Forgotten About in Your Fridge," it would be a dead heat between a half-used onion and a bunch of herbs. The mighty scallion solves both of those problems in a single ingredient. Skip the onions and herbs, and reach for the scallion instead: sauté the white parts for a savory allium backbone and chop up the green parts to use as a fresh garnish.

Tip: If you just plan on using the greens, use the world's most low-lift gardening trick to regrow your scallions by putting the whites, root sides down, in a glass with a couple inches of water and place on a sunny windowsill. After just a few days, green shoots appear like magic.

Chicken Noodle Soup, page 20

← HERBS

Save your stems! While some herb stems (like parsley) can taste bitter when eaten raw, cilantro is different. Sweet, fresh, and potent, the flavor intensifies as you travel down the stem but never becomes bitter. If a recipe calls for cilantro and a slightly crunchy texture isn't an issue, use the stems as well as the leaves. Making a stock or broth? Toss in parsley stems to impart a vegetal flavor.

Tip: Got a lot of almost-past-their-prime herbs? Turn them into ice cubes. Here's how: Place 2 tablespoons of chopped herbs in each well of an ice cube tray, barely cover with water or oil, and freeze. You can mix and match different herbs, add some lemon zest, or even throw in some minced garlic. Once the cubes are frozen, transfer them to a zipper-lock freezer bag and keep them stored in the freezer. Add these flavor-bomb cubes to pan sauces or soups, or defrost them to drizzle over tacos or fluff into rice pilaf.

INGREDIENTS THAT ARE MORE THAN THEY SEEM

We've got more than a few tricks up our sleeves to push the limits of what an ingredient can be, whether that's building layers of flavor or transforming it into something new altogether. We pulled out all the stops in this book, looking for ways to amp things up using the limited amount of ingredients in the recipe—no extras or add-ons, no exceptions. Here were some of our favorites:

- Toast pasta such as **fideos** (*or couscous!*) in oil before you add water to bring out a nutty aroma (Fideos with Shrimp and Fennel, page 144).

- Mix **quinoa** into meatballs for a fluffy texture and extra hit of protein (Lemony Chicken Meatballs with Quinoa and Carrots, page 52).

- Reduce a can of **coconut milk** until the just the fat is left behind and the coconut solids become browned and toasted, and turn it into a superflavorful sauce (Coconut Rice Noodles with Shrimp and Snow Peas, page 146).

- Blend up a bit of **tofu** into soup for an ultracreamy base (Gingery Coconut Carrot Soup with Tofu Croutons, page 165).

Save-the-Shells Shrimp Stock

MAKES: 2 CUPS

If you've already gone through the trouble of painstakingly peeling your shrimp, don't get rid of the shells—use them to make a flavorful stock (yet another reason to buy them with their peels still intact).

Heat 1 tablespoon oil in large saucepan over high heat until shimmering. Add shrimp shells (harvested from 1 pound of shrimp) and cook, stirring frequently, until spotty brown, 2 to 4 minutes. Carefully add 2 cups water and ¼ teaspoon table salt, scraping up any browned bits, and bring to boil. Reduce heat to low and simmer for 5 minutes. Strain stock through fine-mesh strainer set over large bowl, pressing on solids to extract as much liquid as possible; discard solids and reserve stock. Use stock for seafood soups, stews, fideos, risottos, or anything that needs a little briny boost.

Just Buy Something

When you're looking to add lots of flavor while still keeping your ingredient list streamlined, sometimes the best solution is to simply open up a jar. We used store-bought items throughout this book, from premade products that are just as good as homemade (like pizza dough) to condiments that pack a punch (like gochujang and whole-grain mustard). Read on for our favorite ways to amp up your weeknight cooking, without creating more work for yourself.

RULES OF THUMB FOR THE GROCERY AISLE

Start strong with an already-seasoned product

One of our favorite strategies for a no-brainer flavor boost is to buy an ingredient that's already flavored. Sure, you could add your own herbs and spices to bread crumbs, but why not go for seasoned panko instead (see page 155)? Choose garlic hummus instead of plain (see page 52), and go all out with marinated feta (see page 180). We even gravitate towards Boursin Garlic & Fine Herbs cheese as a way to add creaminess, herbs, and alliums in one package (see page 192).

Check the label

When contemplating a jarred product, take a peek at what's actually in it. Choose the product that has a (relatively) short ingredient list with things you recognize and that sound like food. If it's filled with preservatives, stabilizers, and other unpronounceable additives, steer clear.

Take a no-rules approach

Get creative and use premade ingredients for more than just what their instructions say—think about them as ingredients themselves. Used to tossing jarred pesto with pasta and calling it a day? Instead, thin it out and turn it into a dressing for a grilled bread salad (see page 206). You can do more than dip your chips into tomatillo salsa—use it to add bright tanginess to a rich and hearty stew (see page 59). Even put your own spin on instant ramen by keeping the noodles but ditching the seasoning packet (see page 57).

Rotisserie chicken

Rotisserie chicken is the time-saving hero of our weeknight meals. (And money-saving: It's actually cheaper than buying a whole uncooked chicken at most grocery stores.) But instead of carving it and serving it with some sides (snooze), shred it and turn it into an entirely different dinner altogether—from a hearty chopped salad (page 22) to a garlicky pasta (page 129). And don't get rid of the carcass once you're finished—for a quick chicken stock, add it to a pot with half an onion, a couple of bay leaves, and 5 cups of water and simmer for 30 to 45 minutes.

Doughs

We found that store-bought pizza dough is just as good as what you'd make at home, and the same goes for the more-work-than-it's-worth puff pastry—save yourself the headache and just buy it frozen! Then, pile that frozen puff pastry high with butternut squash and shallots for a savory tart (page 192). Or transform store-bought pizza dough into cheesy broccoli calzones (page 195) or an unexpected potato and goat cheese pizza (page 191) for 'za night without the delivery fees.

The Flavor-Bomb Pantry

(ingredients that pack a punch)

Your pantry is probably already filled with staples like baking supplies and canned beans, but there are key flavor-boosting ingredients that will help you level up your meals without a lot of added ingredients. Here are our recommendations for what you should keep on hand to keep your cooking exciting.

PICKLED AND JARRED VEGETABLES

When a dish feels flat, adding salt or acid can frequently be the solution. Brined and pickled vegetables hit both of those factors, and they keep forever. And don't forget about the liquid—it's almost as valuable as the ingredient itself (see "Pickle-y Things," page 9).

- Banana pepper rings
- Capers
- Giardiniera
- Kalamata olives
- Kimchi
- Oil-packed sun-dried tomatoes
- Pickled jalapeños
- Pepperoncini
- Roasted red peppers

OILS AND VINEGARS

There's a whole world beyond vegetable oil and wine vinegars. Keep these around for concentrated flavor in an instant.

- Coconut oil
- Extra-virgin olive oil
- Toasted sesame oil
- Apple cider vinegar
- Balsamic vinegar
- Chinese black vinegar
- Seasoned (or unseasoned) rice vinegar

HERB AND SPICE BLENDS

When you're after a heavy dose of flavor and a wide variety of spices without juggling (or buying) multiple jars, look no further than spice blends. But not all blends are created equal. We like these because they're mainstays in cuisines around the world (no gimmicky single-use spices here), and are useful both for their flavor power as well as versatility.

- Curry powder
- Garam masala
- Herbes de Provence
- Italian seasoning
- Ras el hanout
- Shichimi togarashi
- Za'atar

SAUCES, PASTES, AND CONDIMENTS

We like to think of premade sauces as an ideal combo of ingredients that someone already did the legwork to make delicious. Whether it's barbecue sauce slathered on ribs (see page 231) or hoisin adding a sticky-sweet glaze to pork tenderloin (see page 80), use these for a meal-in-minutes weeknight approach.

- Barbecue sauce
- Black bean garlic sauce
- Chipotle chile in adobo sauce
- Fish sauce
- Gochujang
- Harissa
- Hoisin sauce
- Peanut butter
- Pesto
- Ponzu
- Soy sauce
- Thai red curry paste
- Tomatillo salsa
- Whole-grain mustard
- White miso

Get Saucy

Whip up these supersimple sauces using just a couple store-bought ingredients.

Pantry Peanut Sauce
MAKES: ½ CUP
Whisk ¼ cup creamy peanut butter, 5 tablespoons warm water, and 1 teaspoon Thai red curry paste together in bowl until smooth.

Hummus Sauce
MAKES: ⅔ CUP
Whisk ½ cup garlic hummus, 2½ tablespoons lemon juice, and 4 teaspoons extra-virgin olive oil together in bowl.

Spiced Yogurt Sauce
MAKES: ½ CUP
Whisk ½ cup plain whole-milk yogurt, ½ teaspoon spice blend like garam masala or curry powder, ¼ teaspoon grated lemon zest, and ⅛ teaspoon salt together in bowl.

Use It Up

Popped open a jar but didn't use the whole thing? Never fear. Use this handy chart to finish whatever you've opened up.

INGREDIENT	RECIPE	PAGE
Cheeses		
Blue cheese or Gorgonzola	Blue Cheese, Walnut, and Chicken Chopped Salad	22
	Rosemary Steak Tips with Gorgonzola Polenta	65
Boursin	Thanksgiving-ish Calzones	29
	Creamy Egg Noodles with Pork	133
	Rustic Butternut Squash and Spinach Tart	192
	Grilled Flatbread with Kale and Apples	242
Marinated feta	Shrimp with Warm Barley Salad	122
	Lemony Zoodles with Artichokes, Feta, and Pine Nuts	180
Herbed goat cheese	Broccoli and Goat Cheese Frittata	183
	Grilled Pork Tenderloin Steaks with Grilled Peach and Arugula Salad	224
Condiments and Sauces		
Barbecue sauce	Grilled Ribs with Spicy Slaw	231
	Grilled Barbecue Tempeh Skewers	247
Chipotle chile in adobo sauce	Smoky Pork and Hominy Soup	73
	Chipotle Shrimp Risotto	121
	Black Bean Soup	160
	Loaded Sweet Potatoes	187
Fish sauce	Garlicky Fried Rice with Bok Choy	172
Gochujang	Pork Chops with Gochujang Brussels Sprouts	77
	Kimchi and Ham Steak Fried Rice	93
Harissa	Harissa-Rubbed Chicken with Potatoes and Fennel	36
	Grilled Steak Tips with Sweet Potatoes, Scallions, and Harissa Sauce	214
Pesto	Pan-Seared Strip Steaks with Crispy Potatoes	68
	Grilled Bread Salad with Chicken and Bell Peppers	206
	Grilled Vegetable Platter with Pesto	241
Ponzu	Almost-Instant Ginger Beef Ramen	57
	Sesame-Crusted Tuna with Gingery Bok Choy	116
Seasoned rice vinegar	Salmon and Rice with Cucumber Salad	103
	Chili-Crisp Steak with Rice Noodles	140
	Grilled Strip Steaks with Smashed Cucumber Salad	220
Sesame oil	Salmon and Rice with Cucumber Salad	103
	Grilled Salmon with Charred Red Cabbage Slaw	234

Chicken Every Way

With three kids, cold season hits my family pretty hard. When one (or more) of us is feeling under the weather, I make a big batch of chicken noodle soup. For some fast, from-scratch comfort, I use the bones and skin from a store-bought rotisserie chicken to build the broth, and then shred the meat to add to the finished soup. It may seem odd to include the chicken skin in the broth, but because the bird has already been seasoned and roasted, that's where the all the flavor is. As for the rest, I like to keep it classic with celery, carrots, egg noodles, and chopped parsley.

—RUSSELL SELANDER, *Test Cook*

Chicken Noodle Soup

SERVES 4 TO 6   TOTAL TIME: 1 HOUR

1   (2½-pound) rotisserie chicken, skin and bones reserved, meat shredded into bite-size pieces (3 cups)

10 parsley or dill stems, plus ¼ cup chopped fresh parsley or dill

2   carrots, peeled and cut into ½-inch pieces

2   celery ribs, cut into ½-inch pieces

4   ounces (2 cups) egg noodles

STAPLE INGREDIENTS:

Table salt
Pepper

1. Bring 8 cups water, reserved chicken skin and bones, and parsley stems to simmer in Dutch oven over medium-high heat. Cover, reduce heat to medium-low, and simmer gently for 30 minutes.

2. Using tongs, discard any large pieces of chicken bones. Strain broth through fine-mesh strainer into large bowl, pressing on solids to extract as much broth as possible. Discard solids then return broth to now-empty pot.

3. Bring broth to simmer over medium-high heat, then stir in carrots, celery, 1 teaspoon salt, and ½ teaspoon pepper and cook for 5 minutes. Stir in noodles and cook until noodles and vegetables are tender, about 8 minutes. Stir in shredded chicken and chopped parsley and cook until warmed through, about 2 minutes. Season with salt and pepper to taste and serve.

YOU CAN SERVE WITH

**CRUSTY BREAD
OR CRACKERS**

What can beat a 10-minute dinner? For this fast and funky-in-a-good-way salad, I like to do more than just crumble blue cheese on top, so I melt some into the vinaigrette (just a few seconds in the microwave) to make a smooth, tangy dressing that perfectly coats every bite of crispy romaine lettuce, toasty walnuts, and succulent chicken. A crumble of the remaining blue cheese gives this salad a final flavor boost and provides a supersatisfying creamy texture. You can use a store-bought rotisserie chicken here or poach your own chicken breasts (see page 253).

—LEAH COLINS, *Test Cook*

Blue Cheese, Walnut, and Chicken Chopped Salad

SERVES 4 TOTAL TIME: 10 MINUTES

2 ounces blue cheese or Gorgonzola cheese, crumbled (½ cup), divided

3 tablespoons sherry vinegar or red wine vinegar

3 cups shredded cooked chicken

1 large head romaine lettuce (14 ounces), cut into 1-inch pieces

1 cup walnuts or pecans, toasted and chopped

STAPLE INGREDIENTS:

Extra-virgin olive oil
Table salt
Pepper

1. Microwave ¼ cup olive oil and ¼ cup blue cheese in large bowl until cheese is softened, about 30 seconds. Whisk in vinegar until combined.

2. Add chicken, lettuce, walnuts, and remaining ¼ cup blue cheese to bowl and gently toss to combine. Season with salt and pepper to taste. Serve.

Briny, pickle-y giardiniera is a great way to get a variety of veggies and in-your-face flavor in just one jar (plus it's pantry friendly). I make a thick, hearty vinaigrette out of whole-grain mustard and the zippy giardiniera brine, then chop the pickled vegetables to toss with shredded chicken and red leaf lettuce. Red grapes balance out the spiciness of the giardiniera with a bit of sweetness and help hit this year-round summery dinner salad out of the park. You can use a store-bought rotisserie chicken here or poach your own chicken breasts (see page 253).

—LEAH COLINS, *Test Cook*

Chicken Salad with Whole-Grain Mustard Vinaigrette

SERVES 4   TOTAL TIME: 15 MINUTES

¼ cup whole-grain mustard

¾ cup coarsely chopped jarred giardiniera plus 2 teaspoons giardiniera liquid

1 head red leaf lettuce (12 ounces) or romaine lettuce (12 ounces), cut into 1-inch pieces

3 cups shredded cooked chicken

1 cup red grapes, halved

STAPLE INGREDIENTS:

Extra-virgin olive oil
Table salt
Pepper

1. Whisk mustard, giardiniera liquid, ⅛ teaspoon salt, and ⅛ teaspoon pepper together in large bowl. Whisking constantly, slowly drizzle in 3 tablespoons olive oil until incorporated.

2. Add lettuce, chicken, grapes, and giardiniera to vinaigrette and gently toss to combine. Season with salt and pepper to taste. Serve.

This tart has it all: greens, chicken, and plenty of cheesy goodness. But my favorite part is that there's no need to worry about perfection—it's rustic, after all (no tart tin needed). Layer the spinach, brie, and chicken filling (warmed briefly in the microwave to give the cheese a melty head start) into store-bought pie dough (sure you could make it yourself, but it's a weeknight!) and top it with pieces of the Brie rind for a showstopping look. You can use a store-bought rotisserie chicken here or poach your own chicken breasts (see page 253).

—RUSSELL SELANDER, *Test Cook*

Rustic Chicken Tart with Spinach and Brie

SERVES 4   TOTAL TIME: 40 MINUTES

2   cups shredded cooked chicken

8   ounces frozen chopped spinach, thawed and squeezed dry

6   ounces firm Brie cheese (2 ounces chopped fine, 4 ounces cut into 1-inch pieces)

¼   cup walnuts or pecans, toasted and chopped

1   (9-inch) store-bought pie dough round

STAPLE INGREDIENTS:

Table salt
Pepper

1. Adjust oven rack to middle position and heat oven to 475 degrees. Line rimmed baking sheet with parchment paper. Microwave chicken, spinach, ¼ cup water, finely chopped Brie, ¼ teaspoon salt, and ⅛ teaspoon pepper in covered bowl until warmed through, about 1 minute. Stir walnuts into chicken mixture to combine and season with salt and pepper to taste.

2. Place pie dough round in center of prepared sheet. Spread chicken mixture evenly over dough, leaving 1-inch border around edge. Fold 1-inch edge of dough over filling, pleating every 2 to 3 inches. Gently pinch pleated dough to secure. Arrange remaining Brie pieces over top of filling, with rind facing up. Bake tart until crust is golden and cheese is melted, about 15 minutes, rotating halfway through baking.

3. Transfer sheet to wire rack and let cool for 5 minutes. Serve.

This calzone is like a warm, day-after-Thanksgiving sandwich you don't have to wait all year for. Instead of picking through leftovers, mix shredded chicken with dried cranberries (which plump up as they cook) and two kinds of cheese: herb- and garlic–packed Boursin and tangy, gooey sharp cheddar. Tuck the filling into rounds of store-bought pizza dough (letting it come to room temperature makes it much easier to roll out) and slide them into the oven for a much better than straight-from-the-fridge leftover sandwich. You'll need a light dusting of flour to roll out the dough. You can use a store-bought rotisserie chicken here or poach your own chicken breasts (see page 253).

—RUSSELL SELANDER, *Test Cook*

Thanksgiving-ish Calzones

SERVES 4   TOTAL TIME: 45 MINUTES

1   pound pizza dough, room temperature, split into 4 pieces

2   cups shredded cooked chicken

8   ounces cheddar cheese, shredded (2 cups)

1   (5.2-ounce) package Boursin Garlic & Fine Herbs cheese, crumbled (1 cup)

⅓   cup dried cranberries

STAPLE INGREDIENTS:

Extra-virgin olive oil
Table salt
Pepper

1. Adjust oven rack to middle position and heat oven to 475 degrees. Line rimmed baking sheet with aluminum foil and brush foil with 1 tablespoon olive oil. Place one dough piece on clean counter and, using your cupped hand, drag in small circles until dough feels taut and round. Repeat with remaining dough pieces and cover loosely with plastic wrap. Combine chicken, cheddar, Boursin, cranberries, ½ teaspoon pepper, and ¼ teaspoon salt in bowl; set aside.

2. Working on lightly floured counter, press and roll 1 piece of reserved dough (keep remaining pieces covered) into 8-inch round of even thickness. Repeat with remaining dough pieces. Working with 1 dough round at a time (keep remaining pieces covered), spread one quarter of chicken mixture evenly over half of dough round, leaving 1-inch border at edge. Fold top half of dough over filling and crimp edges to seal. Gently transfer to prepared sheet and repeat with remaining dough rounds and filling.

3. Using sharp knife, cut two 1-inch steam vents on top of each calzone, then brush tops evenly with 1 tablespoon olive oil. Bake until golden brown, 18 to 22 minutes, rotating halfway through baking.

4. Transfer sheet to wire rack and let calzones cool for 5 minutes. Serve.

When I was a kid, chicken cordon bleu seemed like the epitome of luxury—the French-sounding name, the tightly rolled pinwheels, the stretchy cheese when you cut into it. Now it might be a bit out of style, but those flavors never get old (same goes for grilled ham and cheese sandwiches). That's why this supersimple dinner is in regular rotation in my weeknight cooking; it's like chicken cordon bleu without the fuss. Best of all? There's still that ultimate cheese pull.

—BRENNA DONOVAN, *Editor*

Prosciutto-Wrapped Chicken with Asparagus

SERVES 4   TOTAL TIME: 40 MINUTES

4 **(6- to 8-ounce) boneless, skinless chicken breasts, trimmed and pounded to ½-inch thickness**

8 **thin slices prosciutto (4 ounces)**

4 **ounces fontina cheese, cut into 4 slices**

2 **pounds asparagus, trimmed**

2 **shallots, halved and sliced thin**

STAPLE INGREDIENTS:

**Extra-virgin olive oil
Table salt
Pepper**

1. Adjust oven rack to middle position and heat oven to 350 degrees. Line rimmed baking sheet with parchment paper. Pat chicken dry with paper towels and sprinkle with ¼ teaspoon pepper. Wrap each breast with 2 slices prosciutto.

2. Heat 1 tablespoon olive oil in 12-inch ovensafe nonstick skillet over medium-high heat until just smoking. Add chicken and cook until prosciutto is lightly browned, about 2 minutes per side. Transfer to prepared sheet and top each breast with 1 slice fontina. Bake until chicken registers 160 degrees, 12 to 15 minutes. Transfer chicken to serving platter, tent loosely with aluminum foil, and let rest for 5 minutes.

3. Meanwhile, heat 1 tablespoon olive oil in now-empty skillet over medium-high heat until shimmering. Add asparagus and cook until just tender and spotty brown, about 4 minutes. Add shallots, ¼ teaspoon salt, and ⅛ teaspoon pepper and cook until shallots are lightly browned, about 2 minutes. Serve asparagus with chicken.

One key to building flavor with just five ingredients? It's all about the fond, those yummy browned bits on the bottom of the pan. Sear chicken breasts first and then, while they rest, sauté cherry tomatoes in the same skillet before deglazing the pan (with water!) to create a flavorful cooking liquid without any broth. Bulgur then soaks up all of the chickeny, tomatoey flavors in a mere five minutes. To finish, just toss a few more easy-to-prep ingredients—salty kalamata olives and crumbled feta—into the pilaf for a speedy and delicious one-pan dinner.

—LEAH COLINS, *Test Cook*

Pan-Seared Chicken with Warm Bulgur Pilaf

SERVES 4   TOTAL TIME: 30 MINUTES

4 (6- to 8-ounce) boneless, skinless chicken breasts, trimmed and pounded to ½-inch thickness

10 ounces cherry tomatoes, halved

1 cup fine-grind bulgur

4 ounces feta cheese, crumbled (1 cup)

½ cup pitted kalamata olives, halved

STAPLE INGREDIENTS:

Extra-virgin olive oil
Table salt
Pepper

1. Pat chicken dry with paper towels and sprinkle with ½ teaspoon salt and ¼ teaspoon pepper. Heat 1 tablespoon olive oil in 12-inch nonstick skillet over medium-high heat until just smoking. Add chicken and cook until golden brown and registers 160 degrees, 6 to 8 minutes per side. Transfer to cutting board, tent loosely with aluminum foil, and let rest while cooking bulgur.

2. Meanwhile, add tomatoes to skillet and cook until skins blister and begin to release their juices, 1 to 2 minutes. Stir in 1½ cups water and bring to boil, scraping up any browned bits. Stir in bulgur and ½ teaspoon salt. Cover, remove from heat, and let sit for 5 minutes.

3. Fluff bulgur with fork and stir in feta, olives, and 2 tablespoons olive oil. Season with salt and pepper to taste. Slice chicken and serve with bulgur pilaf, drizzling with olive oil to taste.

There are few things I love more than crispy-skinned roast chicken, especially as the weather turns colder. This recipe is my go-to: It's so simple and makes my kitchen smell just like a classic roast chicken, but no trussing or whole-bird wrangling required. The parsnips roast underneath the chicken, soaking up the drippings in the oven. Then, any extra rendered fat transforms into a gravy-like sauce on the stovetop with a little help from fresh rosemary and honey. One thing I don't love? Dishes. Luckily, just one ovensafe skillet makes the transition between stovetop and oven streamlined and keeps cleanup to a minimum.

—BRENNA DONOVAN, *Editor*

Roasted Chicken with Honey-Glazed Parsnips

SERVES 4   TOTAL TIME: 50 MINUTES

4   (10- to 12-ounce) bone-in split chicken breasts, trimmed and halved crosswise

2   pounds parsnips or carrots, peeled and cut into 3-inch-long by ¾-inch-wide pieces

3   tablespoons honey

1   tablespoon minced fresh rosemary or 1 teaspoon dried

STAPLE INGREDIENTS:

Vegetable oil
Table salt
Pepper

1. Adjust oven rack to middle position and heat oven to 450 degrees. Pat chicken dry with paper towels and sprinkle with ½ teaspoon salt and ¼ teaspoon pepper. Heat 2 tablespoons vegetable oil in ovensafe 12-inch skillet over medium-high heat until just smoking. Add chicken skin side down and cook until skin is crispy and golden, about 4 minutes. Transfer to plate.

2. Add parsnips to now-empty skillet and cook until lightly browned, about 3 minutes. Nestle chicken skin side up in parsnips then transfer skillet to oven. Roast until chicken registers 160 degrees and parsnips are almost tender, about 20 minutes.

3. Carefully remove hot skillet from oven. Transfer chicken to serving platter, tent loosely with aluminum foil, and let rest for 5 minutes. While chicken rests, add honey and rosemary to parsnips in skillet and cook over medium heat until liquid has thickened to glaze, about 3 minutes. Transfer glazed parsnips to platter with chicken, drizzle with any remaining glaze in skillet, and serve.

YOU CAN SERVE WITH

**QUINOA, RICE,
CRUSTY BREAD, OR
A SIMPLE SALAD**

Harissa, the smoky, spicy North African chile paste, adds a heavy dose of flavor to anything it touches. Recipes vary depending on region, with differing ratios of chiles and warm spices like coriander, cumin, and caraway. Here, it becomes almost two different ingredients. When rubbed on chicken and roasted, it turns into a concentrated glaze; when whisked together with lemon and oil, it's the spicy hit in a bright, punchy vinaigrette. I couldn't ask for a better (or easier!) sheet-pan dinner.

—BRENNA DONOVAN, *Editor*

Harissa-Rubbed Chicken with Potatoes and Fennel

SERVES 4   TOTAL TIME: 45 MINUTES

2 fennel bulbs, 1 tablespoon fronds minced, stalks discarded, bulbs halved, cored, and cut into 1-inch wedges

1 pound Yukon gold potatoes, peeled and sliced crosswise into ½-inch-thick rounds

4 (10- to 12-ounce) bone-in split chicken breasts, trimmed and halved crosswise

¼ cup harissa paste, divided

1 teaspoon grated lemon zest plus 1 tablespoon juice

1. Adjust oven rack to lowest position and heat oven to 475 degrees. Toss fennel wedges, potatoes, 2 tablespoons olive oil, ½ teaspoon salt, and ¼ teaspoon pepper together on rimmed baking sheet then arrange in single layer.

2. Pat chicken dry with paper towels and rub all over with 3 tablespoons harissa and sprinkle with ½ teaspoon salt and ¼ teaspoon pepper. Place chicken skin-side up on top of vegetables on sheet. Roast until vegetables are beginning to brown on bottom and breasts register 160 degrees, 25 to 30 minutes.

3. Remove sheet from oven, tent chicken and vegetables loosely with aluminum foil, and let rest for 5 minutes. Whisk minced fennel fronds, remaining 1 tablespoon harissa, lemon zest and juice, 3 tablespoons olive oil, and ¼ teaspoon salt together in bowl. Serve chicken and vegetables with harissa sauce.

STAPLE INGREDIENTS:

Extra-virgin olive oil
Table salt
Pepper

Black bean garlic sauce, made from fermented black soybeans, garlic, and spices, is an umami-rich powerhouse ingredient (with a long shelf life) that's full of salty, sweet, and slightly funky flavors. It's the shining star of this stir-fry—I thin it out with water and a bit of soy sauce and use it as a marinade for the chicken as well as a finishing sauce. Scallion whites help build the aromatic base and a bag of frozen veggies (you can really use any you have on hand) plus the remaining scallion greens bring this dead-simple stir-fry to life.

—LEAH COLINS, *Test Cook*

Stir-Fried Chicken and Vegetables with Black Bean Garlic Sauce

SERVES 4   TOTAL TIME: 35 MINUTES

⅓ cup black bean garlic sauce

2 tablespoons soy sauce

1½ pounds boneless skinless chicken thighs, trimmed and sliced ¼ inch thick

1 pound frozen stir-fry vegetable blend, thawed

6 scallions, whites sliced thin and greens cut into 1-inch pieces, separated

STAPLE INGREDIENT:
Vegetable oil

1. Whisk black bean sauce, ¼ cup water, and soy sauce together in bowl. Measure 3 tablespoons sauce mixture into medium bowl, then stir in chicken and let sit for 10 minutes. Set aside remaining sauce mixture.

2. Heat 1½ teaspoons vegetable oil in 12-inch nonstick skillet over high heat until just smoking. Add half of chicken, breaking up any clumps, and cook until cooked through, 3 to 5 minutes; transfer to bowl. Repeat with 1½ teaspoons oil and remaining chicken.

3. Heat 2 teaspoons oil in now-empty skillet over high heat until shimmering. Add stir-fry vegetables and cook for 30 seconds. Stir in 2 tablespoons water then cover skillet, reduce heat to medium, and cook until vegetables are crisp-tender, 1 to 3 minutes. Push vegetables to sides of skillet. Add scallion whites and 1 teaspoon oil to center and cook, mashing scallion whites into skillet, until fragrant, about 1 minute; stir into vegetables.

4. Stir chicken and any accumulated juices into skillet with vegetables. Whisk remaining sauce mixture to recombine, then add to skillet and cook, stirring constantly, until sauce is slightly thickened, about 1 minute. Stir in scallion greens and serve.

Curry powder is not at all traditional in Indian cooking: It's actually a British invention, a hodgepodge of spices that usually includes turmeric along with anything from garlic, ginger, and cinnamon to cumin, fennel seed, and coriander. But the sheer number of spices in the mix means it's a great way to add lots of flavor with just a single ingredient. Here, it's bloomed in the skillet with a bit of oil, then coats pieces of chicken. Tomato sauce and okra, with its natural thickening properties, round out the sauce. Fresh is best, but you can substitute 4 cups of frozen cut okra if that's all you can find (just be sure to thaw it and thoroughly pat it dry first).

—BRENNA DONOVAN, *Editor*

Curried Chicken with Okra

SERVES 4   TOTAL TIME: 40 MINUTES

1½ pounds boneless, skinless chicken thighs, trimmed and cut into 1-inch pieces

2 tablespoons curry powder

1 (15-ounce) can tomato sauce

12 ounces okra, stemmed and cut into ½-inch pieces

¼ cup chopped fresh cilantro

STAPLE INGREDIENTS:

Vegetable oil
Table salt
Pepper

---

1. Pat chicken dry with paper towels and sprinkle with ½ teaspoon salt and ¼ teaspoon pepper. Heat 1 tablespoon vegetable oil in 12-inch nonstick skillet over medium-high heat until just smoking. Add chicken and cook, stirring occasionally, until lightly browned, 6 to 8 minutes.

2. Push chicken to sides of skillet. Add 2 tablespoons oil, ¼ teaspoon salt, and curry powder to center and cook until fragrant, about 30 seconds. Stir curry mixture to coat chicken, then stir in tomato sauce and 1 cup water and bring to simmer.

3. Stir in okra and continue to simmer over medium-high heat until sauce is thickened and chicken is cooked through, about 10 minutes. Season with salt and pepper to taste and sprinkle with cilantro. Serve.

YOU CAN SERVE WITH
RICE, ROTI, OR NAAN

Whole cumin seeds lend toasty, woodsy flavor as well as crunchy texture to this updated take on standard chicken and rice. You start by searing the thighs skin side down and then sprinkling them with cumin seeds before putting them in the oven. This way, the seeds become pleasantly toasted without any bitter burned bite. Then, take advantage of that rendered chicken fat in the pan by cooking the cauliflower in it along with some more cumin seeds—the tiny pieces of cauliflower "couscous" soak up all the savory flavor. A finale of chopped fresh mint and lime zest brings a welcome brightness.

—LEAH COLINS, *Test Cook*

Cumin-Spiced Chicken Thighs with Cauliflower Couscous

SERVES 4   TOTAL TIME: 40 MINUTES

8   (5- to 7-ounce) bone-in chicken thighs, trimmed

4   teaspoons cumin seeds, divided

1   head cauliflower (2 pounds), cored and cut into ½-inch pieces

½   cup plus 2 tablespoons chopped fresh mint, divided

1½   teaspoons grated lime zest, plus lime wedges for serving

STAPLE INGREDIENTS:

Vegetable oil
Table salt
Pepper

1. Adjust oven rack to upper-middle position and heat oven to 375 degrees. Pat chicken dry with paper towels and sprinkle with ½ teaspoon salt and ¼ teaspoon pepper. Heat 1 tablespoon vegetable oil in 12-inch nonstick skillet over medium-high heat until just smoking. Add chicken, skin side down, and cook until well browned, 7 to 10 minutes.

2. Transfer chicken, skin side up, to rimmed baking sheet (do not wipe out skillet). Sprinkle chicken with 2 teaspoons cumin seeds and roast until it registers 175 degrees, 15 to 20 minutes. Transfer chicken to large plate, tent loosely with aluminum foil, and let rest for 5 minutes.

3. Meanwhile, working in 2 batches, pulse cauliflower in food processor into ¼- to ⅛-inch pieces, about 6 pulses. Heat 2 tablespoons reserved fat in skillet (or add vegetable oil until it measures 2 tablespoons) over medium-high heat until shimmering. Add cauliflower, remaining 2 teaspoons cumin seeds, ¾ teaspoon salt, and ¾ teaspoon pepper and cook until just tender, 7 to 10 minutes. Off heat, stir in ½ cup mint and lime zest.

4. Sprinkle remaining 2 tablespoons mint over top of chicken and cauliflower and serve with lime wedges.

YOU CAN SERVE WITH

**POLENTA, QUINOA,
OR CRUSTY BREAD**

For this recipe, my flavor-boosting secret isn't necessarily a specific ingredient; it's simply the oven. Roasting fennel and orange slices draws out their natural sweetness and aromatic appeal. While the fennel and orange are in the oven, I sear the chicken thighs on the stovetop to ensure evenly crisped skin before nestling them into the fennel mixture on the baking sheet. Then everything finishes cooking together in the oven. I love the dense, rich flavor and meaty texture of oil-cured black olives, but if you can't find them, substitute any black olive you like.

—LEAH COLINS, *Test Cook*

Chicken Thighs with Fennel, Orange, and Olives

SERVES 4   TOTAL TIME: 40 MINUTES

3 fennel bulbs, 1 tablespoon fronds minced, stalks discarded, bulbs halved, cored, and sliced thin

1 orange, halved lengthwise and sliced thin into half moons

2 garlic cloves, minced

8 (5- to 7-ounce) bone-in chicken thighs, trimmed

½ cup pitted oil-cured black olives, chopped

STAPLE INGREDIENTS:

Extra-virgin olive oil
Table salt
Pepper

1. Adjust oven rack to upper-middle position and heat oven to 475 degrees. Toss fennel, orange, garlic, 2 tablespoons olive oil, and ¼ teaspoon salt together on rimmed baking sheet then arrange in single layer. Roast until fennel begins to soften, 15 to 18 minutes.

2. Meanwhile, pat chicken dry with paper towels and sprinkle with ½ teaspoon salt and ¼ teaspoon pepper. Heat 2 teaspoons oil in 12-inch skillet over medium-high heat until just smoking. Add chicken, skin side down, and cook until well browned, 7 to 10 minutes. Remove from heat.

3. Stir fennel mixture on sheet to recombine, then nestle in chicken, skin side up. Return sheet to oven and roast until chicken registers 175 degrees, 15 to 20 minutes. Transfer chicken to platter, tent loosely with aluminum foil, and let rest for 5 minutes.

4. Meanwhile, toss fennel mixture with olives and season with salt and pepper to taste. Sprinkle with fennel fronds and serve with chicken.

One thing I always have in my fridge is plain whole-milk yogurt. Sometimes I have it for breakfast with granola, or I'll dollop it on tacos in place of sour cream. But more often than not I'm using it as the base of a sauce. This rendition is especially easy: just garam masala, lemon zest, and a bit of salt. It's the perfect creamy, tangy complement to roasted sweet potatoes and warmly spiced chicken. But the real sleeper hit of this recipe is the roasted lemons: They become sweet, caramelized flavor bombs that tie the whole dish together.

—BRENNA DONOVAN, *Editor*

Roasted Chicken and Sweet Potatoes with Garam Masala–Yogurt Sauce

SERVES 4   TOTAL TIME: 45 MINUTES

½   cup plain whole-milk yogurt

2½ teaspoons garam masala, divided

¼   teaspoon grated lemon zest, lemon quartered

2   pounds sweet potatoes, unpeeled, cut lengthwise into 1½-inch-thick wedges

8   (5- to 7-ounce) bone-in chicken thighs, trimmed

STAPLE INGREDIENTS:

Vegetable oil
Table salt
Pepper

1. Adjust oven racks to upper-middle and lower-middle positions and heat oven to 450 degrees. Line rimmed baking sheet with parchment paper. Whisk yogurt, ½ teaspoon garam masala, lemon zest, and ⅛ teaspoon salt together in bowl; set yogurt sauce aside until ready to serve.

2. Toss potatoes, lemon wedges, 2 tablespoons vegetable oil, ½ teaspoon salt, and ½ teaspoon pepper together on prepared sheet then arrange in single layer, placing lemon wedges rind side down. Roast on upper-middle rack until lightly browned and tender, about 30 minutes.

3. Meanwhile, pat chicken dry with paper towels and sprinkle with remaining 2 teaspoons garam masala, ½ teaspoon salt, and ¼ teaspoon pepper. Heat 1 tablespoon oil in ovensafe 12-inch skillet over medium-high heat until just smoking. Add chicken, skin side down, and cook until well browned, 7 to 10 minutes. Flip chicken skin side up, transfer to lower-middle rack in oven, and roast until chicken registers 175 degrees, 20 to 25 minutes.

4. Transfer chicken to large plate, tent loosely with aluminum foil, and let rest for 5 minutes. Serve chicken with roasted potato wedges and lemon and reserved yogurt sauce.

Everything happens in just one skillet here, starting with cooking bacon, then searing chicken pieces in the rendered fat before popping them in the oven to finish cooking. Once the chicken is cooked you'll set it aside to rest, and then the skillet goes back to the stovetop to sauté crunchy, peppery radishes in all the good stuff left behind until they turn roasty and sweet. A whopping 10 cups of spinach (don't freak out, it'll wilt down significantly) gets stirred in just before serving, and it all comes together with the crispy bacon and a spritz of lemon juice to wake everything up.

—BRENNA DONOVAN, *Editor*

Crispy Chicken with Sautéed Radishes, Spinach, and Bacon

SERVES 4   TOTAL TIME: 45 MINUTES

2 slices bacon, chopped fine

3 pounds bone-in chicken pieces (split breasts cut in half crosswise, drumsticks, and/or thighs), trimmed

10 ounces radishes, trimmed and quartered

10 ounces (10 cups) baby spinach

2 teaspoons lemon juice, plus lemon wedges for serving

STAPLE INGREDIENTS:

Table salt
Pepper

1. Adjust oven rack to middle position and heat oven to 450 degrees. Cook bacon in ovensafe 12-inch skillet over medium heat until crispy, 5 to 7 minutes. Using slotted spoon, transfer bacon to paper towel–lined plate, reserving rendered fat in skillet.

2. Pat chicken dry with paper towels and sprinkle with ½ teaspoon salt and ¼ teaspoon pepper. Heat reserved fat in skillet over medium-high heat until just smoking. Add chicken, skin side down, and cook until well browned, 7 to 10 minutes. Flip chicken skin side up, transfer skillet to oven, and roast until breasts register 160 degrees and drumsticks/thighs register 175 degrees, 15 to 20 minutes. Transfer chicken to plate, tent loosely with aluminum foil, and let rest while cooking radishes.

3. Being careful of hot skillet handle, discard all but 1 tablespoon fat from skillet (or add vegetable oil until it measures 1 tablespoon) and return to medium-high heat. Add radishes and ½ teaspoon salt and cook until tender, about 2 minutes. Stir in spinach and cook until wilted, about 2 minutes. Off heat, stir in bacon and lemon juice. Transfer to serving platter and top with chicken. Serve with lemon wedges.

Because I spend my days cooking for a living, when it comes to making dinner for my family I don't like to be fussing about the kitchen doing a lot of hands-on cooking. It's hard to get more hands-off than this recipe. You start by preheating the oven with the sheet pan inside—that way, the fennel-studded Italian chicken sausage and broccoli sizzle when they hit the pan, jump-starting the browning process. While they roast, quick-cooking barley is ready in just moments on the stove. Once everything is cooked, just mix the barley into the roasted broccoli, add some garlic and Parm, and you're in business.

—RUSSELL SELANDER, *Test Cook*

Sheet-Pan Italian Chicken Sausages with Broccoli and Barley

SERVES 4   TOTAL TIME: 40 MINUTES

12 ounces broccoli florets, cut into 1½-inch pieces

1½ pounds fully cooked Italian chicken sausage

1 cup quick-cooking barley

1 ounce Parmesan cheese, grated (½ cup)

1 garlic clove, minced

STAPLE INGREDIENTS:

Extra-virgin olive oil
Table salt
Pepper

1. Adjust oven rack to lowest position and heat oven to 425 degrees. Brush rimmed baking sheet with 1 tablespoon olive oil. Transfer sheet to oven and heat until oil is just smoking, 3 to 5 minutes.

2. Toss broccoli with 2 tablespoons oil, ½ teaspoon salt, and ¼ teaspoon pepper. Arrange sausage and broccoli in single layer on preheated sheet. Roast until sausage is browned on bottom, about 12 minutes. Flip sausage, stir broccoli, and continue to roast until sausage is browned on second side and broccoli is tender, about 12 minutes longer. Transfer sausage to platter and tent loosely with aluminum foil; transfer broccoli to serving bowl.

3. Meanwhile, bring 1½ cups water and ¼ teaspoon salt to boil in medium saucepan. Add barley, cover, reduce heat to low, and cook until tender and most of water is absorbed, about 10 minutes.

4. Add barley, Parmesan, garlic, and 2 tablespoons oil to roasted broccoli in serving bowl, toss gently to combine, and season with salt and pepper to taste. Serve with sausage.

Almost every ingredient pulls double-duty in this no-waste dinner. Fluffy white quinoa (other types are too crunchy) is the base—along with carrots—as well as a way to keep the meatballs tender. Hummus and lemon zest add moisture to the meatballs, and additional hummus is thinned with lemon juice to make a creamy, drizzle-able sauce. Even the carrot tops are used. Be sure to use ground chicken, not ground chicken breast (also labeled 99 percent fat free) here.

—CAMILA CHAPARRO, *Test Cook*

Lemony Chicken Meatballs with Quinoa and Carrots

SERVES 4   **TOTAL TIME: 1¼ HOURS**

1½ cups prewashed white quinoa

¾ cup garlic hummus, divided

1 teaspoon grated lemon zest plus 2½ tablespoons juice

1 pound ground chicken

1 pound carrots with their greens, carrots peeled and sliced thin on bias, ⅓ cup greens chopped

---

STAPLE INGREDIENTS:

Extra-virgin olive oil
Table salt
Pepper

---

1. Cook quinoa in medium saucepan over medium-high heat, stirring frequently, until very fragrant and making continuous popping sounds, 5 to 7 minutes. Stir in 1¾ cups water and ½ teaspoon salt and bring to simmer. Reduce heat to low, cover, and simmer until quinoa is tender and water is absorbed, 18 to 22 minutes, stirring once halfway through cooking. Remove pot from heat and let sit, covered, for 5 minutes, then gently fluff with fork and set aside to cool slightly. Meanwhile, whisk ½ cup hummus, lemon juice, and 4 teaspoons olive oil together in bowl. Season with salt and pepper to taste; set hummus sauce aside until ready to serve.

2. Combine chicken, 1 cup cooled quinoa, lemon zest, ½ teaspoon salt, ¼ teaspoon pepper, and remaining ¼ cup hummus in large bowl. Using wet hands, gently knead until combined. Pinch off and roll mixture into 20 tightly packed 1½-inch-wide meatballs.

3. Heat 3 tablespoons oil in 12-inch nonstick skillet over medium-high heat until shimmering. Add meatballs and cook until well browned and cooked through, 9 to 11 minutes, turning gently as needed. Transfer meatballs to plate and tent loosely with aluminum foil to keep warm.

4. Add carrots, 3 tablespoons water, and ¼ teaspoon salt to now-empty skillet. Cover and cook over medium-high heat for 2 minutes. Uncover and cook until carrots are tender and spotty brown, 3 to 4 minutes. Stir in remaining 3 cups cooled quinoa, reduce heat to medium, and cook until quinoa is warmed through, about 2 minutes. Stir in 1 tablespoon oil and season with salt and pepper to taste. Sprinkle quinoa with carrot greens, drizzle with olive oil to taste, and serve with meatballs and hummus sauce.

Meaty Meals

Instant ramen is the ultimate nostalgic indulgence for me. As a kid, I would have eaten the orange-colored package of Oodles of Noodles every day if it were up to me (sadly, it wasn't). To bring it ever-so-slightly into adulthood, keep the noodle brick but ditch the sodium bomb of a seasoning packet. Start by browning steak tips, and then use the fond to amp up a chicken broth base. A healthy dose of ponzu brings soy and citrus elements, and combined with fresh ginger is the only other seasoning needed. Once the noodles get nice and oodley in the broth, the thinly sliced steak turns this childhood favorite into a hearty meal.

—SAM BLOCK, *Test Cook*

Almost-Instant Ginger Beef Ramen

SERVES 4   TOTAL TIME: 35 MINUTES

1 pound sirloin steak tips, trimmed and cut into 2-inch pieces

6 cups chicken broth

3 tablespoons grated fresh ginger

4 (3-ounce) packages ramen noodles, seasoning packets discarded

3 tablespoons ponzu

STAPLE INGREDIENTS:

Vegetable oil
Table salt
Pepper

1. Pat steak dry with paper towels and sprinkle with ½ teaspoon salt and ½ teaspoon pepper. Heat 1 tablespoon vegetable oil in Dutch oven over medium-high heat until just smoking. Add steak and cook until well browned all over and meat registers 120 to 125 degrees (for medium-rare), 7 to 10 minutes, flipping as needed. Transfer to cutting board, tent loosely with aluminum foil, and let rest while cooking soup.

2. Add broth, 2 cups water, and ginger to now-empty Dutch oven and bring to boil, scraping up any browned bits. Add noodles and cook, stirring often, until tender, about 3 minutes. Off heat, stir in ponzu and any accumulated juices from steak. Slice steak thin and serve with noodles and broth.

YOU CAN SERVE WITH
**TORTILLA CHIPS
OR CRUSTY BREAD**

When sweater-weather season starts up, sometimes a hearty stew is the only thing that will do. My favorite cozy concoction takes inspiration from rich and tangy entomatado de res, a Mexican beef and tomatillo stew. Blade steak has a big, beefy flavor and silky texture similar to traditional chuck-eye roast, but the meat is already sliced pretty thin and requires less prep work—all I have to do is cut the meat into bite-size pieces to ensure a speedy simmer time. Store-bought tomatillo salsa (also known as salsa verde) adds a boost of freshness just by popping open a jar. Canned white beans along with their starchy liquid bring body and richness to the stew.

—LEAH COLINS, *Test Cook*

Beef, Tomatillo, and White Bean Stew

SERVES 4 TO 6   TOTAL TIME: 1 HOUR 5 MINUTES

2   pounds blade steak, trimmed and cut into ½-inch pieces

4   teaspoons ground cumin

2   cups jarred tomatillo salsa, divided

2   (15-ounce) cans cannellini beans, undrained

½   cup plus 2 tablespoons chopped fresh cilantro, divided

STAPLE INGREDIENTS:

Vegetable oil
Table salt
Pepper

1. Pat steak dry with paper towels and sprinkle with ½ teaspoon salt and ¼ teaspoon pepper. Heat 1 tablespoon vegetable oil in Dutch oven over medium-high heat until just smoking. Add steak and cook until beginning to brown, 6 to 10 minutes. Stir in cumin and cook until fragrant, about 1 minute.

2. Stir in 1½ cups salsa and 2 cups water, scraping up any browned bits, and bring to boil. Cover and simmer vigorously for 20 minutes, adjusting heat as needed and stirring occasionally. Stir in beans with their liquid and simmer uncovered until meat is tender and stew is thickened, 25 to 35 minutes. (If stew begins to stick to bottom of pot or looks too thick, stir in extra water.)

3. Off heat stir in ½ cup cilantro and remaining ½ cup salsa. Season with salt and pepper to taste. Sprinkle individual portions with remaining 2 tablespoons cilantro. Serve.

Every time I peruse the spice aisle at my local grocery store, I find another blend to add to my cupboard. Most recently I've been loving shichimi togarashi (sometimes called Japanese seven-spice blend), containing chile peppers, orange zest, sesame seeds, and nori. Sear up a steak, then char some shredded cabbage in the pan (a hot skillet and flavorful fond is a terrible thing to waste, and both add extra interest to the humble crucifer), and sprinkle on this spicy, nutty, citrusy blend to take dinner up a notch. Store-bought blends of shichimi togarashi vary widely in spiciness, use more or less depending on your taste.

—CAMILA CHAPARRO, *Test Cook*

Steak with Shichimi Togarashi Charred Cabbage Salad

SERVES 4   TOTAL TIME: 20 MINUTES

1 (1½-pound) skirt steak, trimmed and cut with grain into 4 pieces

1 small red cabbage (1¼ pounds), halved, cored, and sliced thin

3 scallions, white and green parts separated and sliced thin on bias

1 teaspoon grated lime zest plus 1 tablespoon juice

½–1 teaspoon shichimi togarashi, plus extra for serving

STAPLE INGREDIENTS:

Vegetable oil
Table salt
Pepper

1. Pat steaks dry with paper towels and sprinkle with ½ teaspoon salt and ¼ teaspoon pepper. Heat 1 tablespoon vegetable oil in 12-inch skillet over medium-high heat until just smoking. Add steaks and cook until well browned and meat registers 120 to 125 degrees (for medium-rare), 2 to 3 minutes per side. Transfer steaks to cutting board, tent loosely with aluminum foil, and let rest while cooking cabbage.

2. Add cabbage and scallion whites to now-empty skillet and cook over medium-high heat, without moving, until cabbage is spotty brown, about 2 minutes. Transfer to bowl and toss with scallion greens, lime zest and juice, shichimi togarashi, and ½ teaspoon salt. Slice steaks thin against grain and serve with cabbage salad and extra shichimi togarashi.

When I want a quick and easy punch of flavor, I grab a spice blend like ras el hanout, the North African mix of warm spices like black pepper, cumin, cinnamon, paprika, and turmeric. Sprinkled on steak tips that are quickly seared in a skillet, it creates a fond that then adds depth to couscous that gets cooked in the same pan. Tossing in a few final handfuls of pomegranate seeds and fresh spinach looks beautiful and balances out the rich meat.

—CAMILA CHAPARRO, *Test Cook*

Steak Tips with Ras el Hanout and Couscous

SERVES 4   TOTAL TIME: 25 MINUTES

1½ pounds sirloin steak tips, trimmed and cut into 2-inch pieces

2½ teaspoons ras el hanout, divided

¾ cup couscous

2 ounces (2 cups) baby spinach, chopped

¼ cup pomegranate seeds

STAPLE INGREDIENTS:

Vegetable oil
Table salt
Pepper

1. Pat steak dry with paper towels and sprinkle with 2 teaspoons ras el hanout, ½ teaspoon salt, and ¼ teaspoon pepper. Heat 2 tablespoons vegetable oil in 12-inch nonstick skillet over medium-high heat until just smoking. Add steak and cook until well browned all over and meat registers 120 to 125 degrees (for medium-rare), 7 to 10 minutes, flipping as needed. Transfer to cutting board, tent loosely with aluminum foil, and let rest while cooking couscous.

2. Add 1¼ cups water, couscous, ½ teaspoon salt, and remaining ½ teaspoon ras el hanout to now-empty skillet and bring to boil over medium-high heat. Remove from heat, cover, and let sit until couscous is tender, about 5 minutes.

3. Fluff couscous with fork, stir in spinach and pomegranate seeds, and season with salt and pepper to taste. Slice steak thin and serve with couscous.

Chunks of Gorgonzola soften over steak and melt into hot polenta to tie together this umami-packed dinner that's ready in a flash (instant polenta delivers creamy results in a mere 3 minutes!). Piney, aromatic rosemary brings potency to the whole situation and is a perfect match to the salty, funky Gorgonzola. Grape tomatoes cook superfast at the last minute, just enough to soften but still retain some freshness.

—STEPHANIE PIXLEY, *Editor*

Rosemary Steak Tips with Gorgonzola Polenta

SERVES 4   TOTAL TIME: 25 MINUTES

1   cup instant polenta

1½   pounds sirloin steak tips, trimmed and cut into 2-inch pieces

1   tablespoon coarsely chopped fresh rosemary

10   ounces grape or cherry tomatoes, halved

4   ounces Gorgonzola or blue cheese, crumbled (1 cup)

STAPLE INGREDIENTS:

Vegetable oil
Unsalted butter
Table salt
Pepper

1. Bring 4 cups water to boil in large saucepan. Whisk in polenta, reduce heat to medium-low, and cook until thickened, about 3 minutes. Off heat, stir in 3 tablespoons butter, 1 teaspoon salt, and ½ teaspoon pepper. Cover to keep warm.

2. Meanwhile, pat steak dry with paper towels and sprinkle with rosemary, 1 teaspoon salt, and ½ teaspoon pepper. Heat 1 tablespoon vegetable oil in 12-inch nonstick skillet over medium-high heat until just smoking. Add steak and cook until well browned all over and meat registers 120 to 125 degrees (for medium-rare), 7 to 10 minutes, flipping as needed. Transfer to cutting board, tent loosely with aluminum foil, and let rest for 5 minutes.

3. Melt 1 tablespoon butter in now-empty skillet over medium-high heat. Add tomatoes and ½ teaspoon salt and cook until just softened, about 1 minute. Slice steak thin and serve over polenta with tomatoes and Gorgonzola.

Making roasted garlic butter sounds complicated, but it's fancy in name only. All you have to do is peel some garlic cloves (no chopping required!) and roast them with cauliflower and shallots—the makings of your side dish and garnish all on one sheet pan. Once roasted, the garlic mashes easily into softened butter with a sprinkling of chives for freshness and an extra hit of allium. Dolloped on top of seared steaks, the garlic butter brings a luxurious step up from a simple pat of butter, melting and turning into a sauce that ties the whole dish together.

—STEPHANIE PIXLEY, *Editor*

Strip Steaks with Cauliflower and Roasted Garlic Butter

SERVES 4   TOTAL TIME: 40 MINUTES

1   large head cauliflower
     (3 pounds), cored and cut
     into 1½-inch florets

3   large shallots, peeled and
     quartered through root end

6   garlic cloves, peeled

2   (1-pound) boneless strip
     steaks, 1 to 1½ inches thick,
     trimmed and halved crosswise

1   tablespoon chopped
     fresh chives

STAPLE INGREDIENTS:

Vegetable oil
Unsalted butter
Table salt
Pepper

1. Soften 6 tablespoons butter; set aside. Adjust oven rack to lowest position and heat oven to 425 degrees. Toss cauliflower with shallots, garlic, 2 tablespoons vegetable oil, ½ teaspoon salt, and ½ teaspoon pepper on rimmed baking sheet. Roast until vegetables are tender and lightly browned, about 25 minutes, stirring halfway through roasting.

2. Meanwhile, pat steaks dry with paper towels and sprinkle with ½ teaspoon salt and ¼ teaspoon pepper. Heat 1 tablespoon oil in 12-inch nonstick skillet over medium-high heat until just smoking. Add steaks and cook, flipping every 2 minutes, until exteriors are well browned and meat registers 120 to 125 degrees (for medium-rare), 10 to 12 minutes. Transfer to platter, tent with aluminum foil, and let rest for 5 minutes.

3. Mash reserved softened butter, chives, roasted garlic cloves, ¼ teaspoon salt, and ⅛ teaspoon pepper in bowl with fork until combined. Serve steaks with vegetables and garlic butter.

YOU CAN SERVE WITH
**A SIMPLE SALAD,
RICE, OR QUINOA**

Sometimes the simplest dish is the best, and it's tough to get simpler than this three-ingredient recipe (yes, you read that correctly). The classic combo of steak and potatoes is taken up a notch here—par-cooked potatoes develop a gorgeous crust and act like a sponge, soaking up the meaty, savory fat left in the skillet from cooking strip steaks. A swoosh of store-bought pesto adds brightness to keep things from tipping into too-rich territory.

—BRENNA DONOVAN, *Editor*

Pan-Seared Strip Steaks with Crispy Potatoes

SERVES 4   TOTAL TIME: 50 MINUTES

1½ pounds russet potatoes, unpeeled, cut lengthwise into 1-inch wedges

2 (1-pound) boneless strip steaks, 1 to 1½ inches thick, trimmed and halved crosswise

½ cup pesto

STAPLE INGREDIENTS:

Vegetable oil
Table salt
Pepper

1. Combine potatoes, 1 tablespoon vegetable oil, ¼ teaspoon salt, and ⅛ teaspoon pepper in bowl, cover, and microwave until potatoes begin to soften, 7 to 10 minutes, stirring halfway through; drain well.

2. Pat steaks dry with paper towels and sprinkle with ½ teaspoon salt and ¼ teaspoon pepper. Heat 1 tablespoon oil in 12-inch nonstick skillet over medium-high heat until just smoking. Add steaks and cook, flipping every 2 minutes, until exteriors are well browned and meat registers 120 to 125 degrees (for medium-rare), 10 to 12 minutes. Transfer to platter, tent loosely with aluminum foil, and let rest for 5 minutes.

3. Heat ¼ cup oil in now-empty skillet over medium-high heat until shimmering. Add half of potatoes in single layer and cook until golden brown on both cut sides 3 to 6 minutes per side. Transfer potatoes to paper towel–lined plate and season with salt to taste. Repeat with remaining potatoes.

4. Serve potatoes and steak with pesto.

Cozy up to this rustic soup that gives new meaning to the phrase "meat and potatoes." By starting with browning kielbasa in the Dutch oven, smoky, garlic-forward notes permeate every element of the dish—the sausage is more than just an add-on, it's the foundational flavor here. Delicate leeks soften in the same pot, and a little bit of flour ensures the soup isn't too brothy. Potato-leek soup typically uses starchy russet or Yukon Gold potatoes, but they contribute a gluey texture to the soup when blended. Switching to waxy, low-starch red potatoes adds body without any stodginess.

—STEPHANIE PIXLEY, *Editor*

Hearty Potato Leek Soup with Kielbasa

SERVES 4   TOTAL TIME: 40 MINUTES

8   ounces kielbasa sausage,
    sliced ½ inch thick

2   pounds leeks, white and light
    green parts only, halved
    lengthwise, chopped, and
    washed thoroughly

1   pound red potatoes, unpeeled
    and cut into ¾-inch pieces

1   tablespoon all-purpose flour

4   cups chicken broth

STAPLE INGREDIENTS:

Unsalted butter
Table Salt
Pepper

1. Brown kielbasa on all sides in Dutch oven over medium-high heat, about 5 minutes. Transfer to paper towel–lined plate.

2. Melt 3 tablespoons butter in now-empty pot, then add leeks and potatoes and cook until leeks begin to soften, about 5 minutes. Stir in flour until absorbed, about 1 minute. Slowly whisk in broth and bring to boil. Reduce heat to medium and simmer until vegetables are tender, 10 to 15 minutes.

3. Carefully process 1½ cups soup in blender until smooth, about 1 minute. Return to pot and stir in kielbasa. Season with salt and pepper to taste. Serve.

YOU CAN SERVE WITH
**CRUSTY BREAD OR
A SIMPLE SALAD**

YOU CAN SERVE WITH

**TORTILLAS OR
CRUSTY BREAD**

When he was growing up in Mexico, my husband's favorite comfort food was pozole rojo—a long-simmered, hearty, downright delicious hominy-based soup. For special occasions I'll make it just like he remembers, but for a quick alternative, this supersimple variation quiets his cravings. Country-style boneless pork ribs bring deep flavor, and simmering them in chicken broth creates a rich base to which I add tart canned hominy. While a variety of chiles and seasonings (usually garlic, onion, and oregano) are traditionally used, for my take I use chipotle chiles in adobo to bring layers of complexity and a little heat with just one ingredient.

—LEAH COLINS, *Test Cook*

Smoky Pork and Hominy Soup

SERVES 4 TO 6   TOTAL TIME: 1 HOUR

2 pounds boneless country-style pork ribs, trimmed and cut into 1-inch pieces

2 tablespoons minced canned chipotle chile in adobo sauce

6 cups chicken broth

2 (15-ounce) cans white hominy, rinsed

½ cup plus 2 tablespoons chopped fresh cilantro, divided

STAPLE INGREDIENTS:

Vegetable oil
Table salt
Pepper

1. Pat pork dry with paper towels and sprinkle with ½ teaspoon salt and ¼ teaspoon pepper. Heat 1 tablespoon vegetable oil in Dutch oven over medium-high heat until just smoking. Add pork and cook, without stirring, until fond begins to form on bottom of pot, 4 to 6 minutes. Stir in chipotle and cook until fragrant, about 1 minute.

2. Stir in broth, scraping up any browned bits and bring to boil. Reduce heat to medium-low, cover, and simmer vigorously for 20 minutes, adjusting heat as needed and stirring occasionally. Stir in hominy and simmer uncovered until meat and hominy are tender, 15 to 20 minutes. (If stew begins to stick to bottom of pot or looks too thick, stir in extra water.)

3. Off heat stir in ½ cup cilantro and season with salt and pepper to taste. Sprinkle individual portions with remaining 2 tablespoons cilantro. Serve.

Horseradish might be best known for adding zip to Bloody Marys or balancing out a rich beef tenderloin, but here it adds a zesty punch to sautéed green beans. A spring-like chive and lemon zest compound butter keeps the horseradish beans from tasting too tart (I save some to slather over the pork chops, too). A final squeeze of lemon wakes everything up.

—LEAH COLINS, *Test Cook*

Pork Chops with Horseradish Green Beans

SERVES 4   TOTAL TIME: 35 MINUTES

2   tablespoons minced
    fresh chives

½   teaspoon grated lemon zest
    plus lemon wedges for serving

4   (6- to 8- ounce) boneless
    pork chops, ¾ to 1 inch
    thick, trimmed

1   pound green beans, trimmed
    and halved crosswise

1   tablespoon prepared
    horseradish, drained

STAPLE INGREDIENTS:

Unsalted butter
Vegetable oil
Table salt
Pepper

1. Soften 4 tablespoons butter then mash with chives, lemon zest, and ⅛ teaspoon salt in bowl until combined; set chive butter aside.

2. Pat chops dry with paper towels and cut 2 slits, about 2 inches apart, through fat on edges of each pork chop, then sprinkle with ½ teaspoon salt and ¼ teaspoon pepper. Heat 1 tablespoon vegetable oil in 12-inch skillet over medium-high heat until just smoking. Add pork and cook, flipping every 2 minutes, until well browned and meat registers 140 to 145 degrees, 10 to 14 minutes. Transfer to plate, dollop with half of chive butter, tent loosely with aluminum foil, and let rest while cooking green beans.

3. Heat 1 tablespoon oil in now-empty skillet over medium heat until shimmering. Add green beans, ¼ teaspoon salt, and ⅛ teaspoon pepper and cook, stirring occasionally, until beginning to brown, 3 to 5 minutes. Add ¼ cup water, cover, and cook until green beans are bright green and still crisp, about 2 minutes. Uncover and continue to cook until water evaporates, 1 to 2 minutes.

4. Stir in horseradish and remaining chive butter and cook until green beans are crisp-tender, 1 to 3 minutes. Season with salt and pepper to taste and serve with pork and lemon wedges.

It's not just because I'm a mom that I think you should eat your vegetables. Brussels sprouts may be the poster child for vegetables we loved to hate, but with the right technique—charred quickly in a skillet, like in this recipe—these mini cabbages can be the star of your dinner plate. Here, they shine in a sweet-spicy-salty sauce of gochujang and rice vinegar, which pairs perfectly with succulent pork chops made in the same skillet. A final sprinkle of toasted sesame seeds adds a nutty finish.

—CAMILA CHAPARRO, *Test Cook*

Pork Chops with Gochujang Brussels Sprouts

SERVES 4　　　TOTAL TIME: 35 MINUTES

3　tablespoons gochujang paste or sauce

3　tablespoons unseasoned rice vinegar

4　(8- to 10-ounce) bone-in pork rib chops, ¾ to 1 inch thick, trimmed

1　pound small (1 to 1½ inches in diameter) brussels sprouts, trimmed and halved

2　teaspoons sesame seeds, toasted

STAPLE INGREDIENTS:

Extra-virgin olive oil
Table salt
Pepper

1. Whisk gochujang, vinegar, and ¼ teaspoon salt together in bowl; set aside until ready to serve. Pat chops dry with paper towels and cut 2 slits, about 2 inches apart, through fat on edges of each pork chop, then sprinkle with ½ teaspoon salt and ¼ teaspoon pepper. Heat 1 tablespoon olive oil in 12-inch nonstick skillet over medium-high heat until just smoking. Add pork and cook, flipping every 2 minutes, until well browned on both sides and meat registers 140 to 145 degrees, 10 to 14 minutes. Transfer to serving platter, tent loosely with aluminum foil, and let rest while cooking brussels sprouts.

2. Wipe out now-empty skillet with paper towels. Carefully arrange brussels sprouts in now-empty skillet in single layer, cut sides down, then drizzle with 5 tablespoons oil. Cover skillet, place over medium-high heat, and cook until sprouts are bright green and cut sides have started to brown, about 5 minutes.

3. Uncover and continue to cook until cut sides of sprouts are well browned and tender, 2 to 3 minutes longer, adjusting heat and moving sprouts as needed. Off heat, stir in reserved gochujang mixture and sesame seeds and season with salt to taste. Serve with chops.

I love cabbage in many forms, but more often than not I'm usually defaulting to enjoying it in crunchy slaws. But there are so many more possibilities for this tasty brassica. Like roasting: When a head of cabbage is cut into wedges and roasted, it transforms into a sweet, silky vegetable. Here, the caramelized layers create the perfect nooks and crannies for soaking up a creamy, mustardy sauce, made deeply savory by the fond from browned pork chops. I'm not skipping out on slaws altogether, but this recipe always is a welcome break from the crunch.

—BRENNA DONOVAN, *Editor*

Mustard Pork Chops with Crispy Cabbage

SERVES 4   TOTAL TIME: 40 MINUTES

- 1 small head green cabbage (1¼ pounds), cut through core into 1-inch wedges

- 8 (5- to 7-ounce) bone-in pork rib chops, ½ inch thick, trimmed

- 1 cup chicken broth

- ¼ cup heavy cream

- 2½ tablespoons whole-grain mustard

STAPLE INGREDIENTS:

Vegetable oil
Unsalted butter
Table salt
Pepper

1. Melt 2 tablespoons butter; set aside. Adjust oven rack to upper-middle position and heat oven to 450 degrees. Place cabbage on rimmed baking sheet, drizzle with reserved melted butter, and sprinkle with ⅛ teaspoon salt and pinch pepper. Roast until cabbage is browned around edges, 20 to 25 minutes.

2. Meanwhile, pat chops dry with paper towels and cut 2 slits, about 2 inches apart, through fat on edges of each pork chop, then sprinkle with ½ teaspoon salt and ¼ teaspoon pepper. Heat 2 teaspoons vegetable oil and additional 1 tablespoon butter in 12-inch skillet over high heat until foaming subsides. Add 4 chops to skillet and cook until browned and meat registers 140 to 145 degrees, about 2 minutes per side. Transfer to large plate and tent loosely with aluminum foil. Repeat with remaining 4 chops, adding more oil and butter as needed.

3. Add broth to now-empty skillet and bring to boil, scraping up any browned bits. Reduce heat to medium and simmer until reduced slightly, 4 to 6 minutes. Add cream and simmer until thickened, 2 to 3 minutes. Stir in mustard and season with salt and pepper to taste. Pour sauce over chops and serve with cabbage.

YOU CAN SERVE WITH

**CRUSTY BREAD,
EGG NOODLES,
OR RICE**

Let's be real: Single sheet-pan dinners are the best kind of dinners. In this case, while the pork tenderloin rests I'm roasting off a veggie medley of asparagus and scallions. Hoisin is one of those sauces that has it all going on: sweet, salty, savory, and sticky. Not only do I coat pork tenderloin in the good stuff, but I also make a compound butter with additional hoisin plus a spicy serrano pepper. Some of the hoisin will inevitably fall off the tenderloin in the oven, so this is a great way to remind the dish what it's made of.

—SAM BLOCK, *Test Cook*

Roasted Pork with Asparagus, Scallions, and Hoisin-Serrano Butter

SERVES 4   TOTAL TIME: 40 MINUTES

1   serrano chile, stemmed, seeded, and minced

1   tablespoon plus ¼ cup hoisin sauce, divided

2   (12- to 16-ounce) pork tenderloins, trimmed

1   pound thick asparagus, trimmed

8   scallions, trimmed

STAPLE INGREDIENTS:

Extra-virgin olive oil
Unsalted butter
Table salt
Pepper

1. Soften 4 tablespoons butter then mash with serrano and 1 tablespoon hoisin in bowl until combined; set aside until ready to serve. Adjust oven rack to lower-middle position and heat oven to 450 degrees.

2. Pat pork dry with paper towels and sprinkle with ½ teaspoon pepper. Arrange pork on aluminum foil–lined rimmed baking sheet, side by side without touching, and brush all over with remaining ¼ cup hoisin. Roast until pork registers 135 to 140 degrees, 20 to 24 minutes. Transfer pork to cutting board, tent loosely with foil, and let rest while roasting vegetables.

3. Toss asparagus and scallions with 2 tablespoons olive oil, ½ teaspoon salt, and ½ teaspoon pepper then spread into even layer over now-empty sheet. Roast until vegetables are tender and spotty brown, 8 to 10 minutes.

4. Slice pork into ½-inch-thick slices and serve with vegetables, dolloping with hoisin-serrano butter.

Quick-cooking and versatile pork tenderloin is one of my weeknight go-tos, and here it's turned into crispy, nutty, tangy cutlets by pounding it thin and dredging it in za'atar-spiked breadcrumbs. The recipe was inspired by Michael Solomonov's chicken schnitzel (one of my favorite recipes in his cookbook *Zahav*). Pair with easy-peasy wedges of roasted acorn squash (so tender, go ahead and eat the skin), serve with a schmear of yogurt, and that sounds like dinner to me.

—CAMILA CHAPARRO, *Test Cook*

Crispy Za'atar Pork with Roasted Acorn Squash

SERVES 4   TOTAL TIME: 35 MINUTES

2   small acorn squashes (1 pound each), halved pole to pole, seeded, and cut into 1½-inch wedges

1   (12- to 16-ounce) pork tenderloin, trimmed and cut crosswise into 4 equal pieces

1   cup plain Greek yogurt, divided

1¼ cups panko bread crumbs

2   tablespoons za'atar, plus extra for serving

STAPLE INGREDIENTS:

Extra-virgin olive oil
Table salt
Pepper

1. Adjust oven rack to middle position and heat oven to 475 degrees. Toss squash with 2 tablespoons olive oil, ¼ teaspoon salt, and ⅛ teaspoon pepper in bowl, then arrange cut sides down in single layer on rimmed baking sheet. Roast until squash is tender, 22 to 25 minutes.

2. Meanwhile, stand pork pieces cut side down on cutting board, cover with plastic wrap, and pound to even ¼-inch thickness. Pat cutlets dry with paper towels. Whisk ½ cup yogurt, ¼ cup water, ½ teaspoon salt, and ¼ teaspoon pepper together in shallow dish. Combine panko, za'atar, ½ teaspoon salt, and ¼ teaspoon pepper in second shallow dish. Working with 1 cutlet at a time, dip pork in yogurt mixture, allowing excess to drip off, then coat with panko mixture, pressing gently to adhere. Transfer to large plate.

3. Line second large plate with triple layer of paper towels. Heat 1 cup oil in 12-inch nonstick skillet over medium-high heat until shimmering. Place 2 cutlets in skillet and cook until deep golden brown and cooked through, 2 to 3 minutes per side. Transfer cutlets to prepared plate and repeat with remaining 2 cutlets.

4. Serve cutlets with squash, remaining ½ cup yogurt, and extra za'atar.

In my opinion, anything eaten in a lettuce wrap is considered healthy—it's basically a salad you eat with your hands (right?)—and it certainly doesn't hurt when what you're eating in said lettuce wrap is supersavory and tasty. Thai red curry paste plays the leading role here, providing concentrated flavors of galangal, shallots, lemongrass, and so much more. Vermicelli noodles not only take this from an appetizer to an entree by bulking it up, but also do a great job of soaking up the sauce to ensure ample flavor in every bite.

—SAM BLOCK, *Test Cook*

Red Curry–Pork Lettuce Wraps

SERVES 4   TOTAL TIME: 20 MINUTES

8 ounces rice vermicelli

¼ cup Thai red curry paste

1½ pounds ground pork

1 head green leaf lettuce or Bibb lettuce, leaves separated

1 red bell pepper or jalapeño chile, stemmed, seeded, and sliced thin

STAPLE INGREDIENTS:

Vegetable oil
Table Salt
Pepper

1. Bring 2 quarts water to boil in large saucepan. Off heat, add noodles and let sit, stirring occasionally until tender about 5 minutes. Drain noodles, rinse with cold water, and drain again; set aside.

2. Meanwhile, heat 1 teaspoon vegetable oil in 12-inch nonstick skillet over medium heat until shimmering. Add curry paste and cook until fragrant and beginning to darken, about 2 minutes. Add pork and cook, breaking up meat with wooden spoon, until just beginning to brown, 7 to 9 minutes. Season with salt and pepper to taste.

3. Using slotted spoon, serve pork in lettuce cups with noodles and bell pepper.

It's hard to get more classic than sausage, peppers, and onions—one whiff and I'm instantly transported to a baseball game or a street fair, tucking into a larger-than-life sub piled high with this killer combo. To re-create this experience with a bit more elegance, I introduce smoky fire-roasted tomatoes into the equation and serve it all over rich and buttery stick-to-your-ribs polenta (instant all the way!), which does a excellent job of sopping up the savory sauce.

—SAM BLOCK, *Test Cook*

Polenta with Sausage and Peppers

SERVES 4   TOTAL TIME: 20 MINUTES

1   **cup instant polenta**

1½ **pounds sweet or hot Italian sausage**

1   **red bell pepper, stemmed, seeded, and sliced thin**

1   **small onion, halved and sliced thin**

1   **(14.5-ounce) can fire-roasted diced tomatoes**

STAPLE INGREDIENTS:

Unsalted butter
Table salt
Pepper

---

1. Bring 4 cups water to boil in large saucepan. Whisk in polenta, reduce heat to medium-low, and cook until thickened, about 3 minutes. Off heat, stir in 3 tablespoons butter, ¾ teaspoon salt, and ½ teaspoon pepper. Cover to keep warm.

2. Meanwhile, place sausage in 12-inch nonstick skillet and cook over medium heat until browned all over, 6 to 10 minutes. Increase heat to medium-high, add bell pepper and onion, and cook, stirring occasionally, until vegetables are softened, 4 to 6 minutes. Add tomatoes, ½ cup water, ¼ teaspoon salt, and ¼ teaspoon pepper. Simmer until sausage registers 160 degrees, 4 to 6 minutes.

3. Top polenta with sausage and pepper mixture. Serve.

The appeal of breakfast for dinner is undeniable, but I often want something a bit more exciting than your regular ol' potatoes and eggs for my weeknight supper. I love using sweet potatoes and celery root as a flavorful alternative to plain potatoes. They quickly soften in the microwave before "hashing" in the skillet with Mexican-style chorizo and a Granny Smith apple for a tart-crisp bite. Clear small wells in the center of the skillet and crack eggs directly into the hash for a poached/fried hybrid that delivers luxuriously oozy yolks.

—LEAH COLINS, *Test Cook*

Sweet Potato, Celery Root, and Apple Hash with Sausage and Eggs

SERVES 4   TOTAL TIME: 40 MINUTES

1   pound sweet potatoes, peeled and cut into ½-inch pieces

7   ounces celery root, peeled and cut into ½-inch pieces

1   pound Mexican-style chorizo, casings removed

1   Granny Smith apple, cored and chopped fine

4   large eggs

STAPLE INGREDIENTS:

Unsalted butter
Table salt
Pepper

1. Melt 1 tablespoon butter. In bowl, toss butter with sweet potatoes, celery root, ½ teaspoon salt, and ⅛ teaspoon pepper. Cover and microwave until vegetables are tender, 7 to 10 minutes, stirring halfway through; drain and set aside.

2. Cook chorizo in 12-inch nonstick skillet over medium-high heat, breaking up meat with wooden spoon, until no longer pink, about 4 minutes. Stir in apple and cook until softened and lightly browned, about 4 minutes longer.

3. Stir in microwaved vegetables and use back of spatula to gently pack hash into skillet. Cook undisturbed for 2 minutes. Flip hash, 1 section at a time, and lightly repack into skillet. Repeat flipping process every 2 minutes until hash is browned, 6 to 8 minutes. Season with salt and pepper to taste.

4. Off heat, make 4 shallow wells in hash with back of spoon. Break 1 egg into each well and sprinkle with ¼ teaspoon salt and ⅛ teaspoon pepper. Cover skillet, place over medium-low heat, and cook for 5 to 7 minutes for runny yolks or 7 to 9 minutes for set yolks. Season with salt and pepper to taste and serve.

The humble bean is a frequent hero in our house, coming to the rescue when I need to pull together a quick (but wholesome!) weeknight dinner. When paired with rich 'nduja sausage—a slightly spicy specialty of the southern Italian province of Calabria that packs a punch of umami and a bit of fermented funk—beans reach superhero status, like in this quick dish of creamy cannellini beans and just-tender kale. (I've also used Italian sausage when I can't find 'nduja; you just need to cook it in a bit of oil.) The crispy lacy edges of a fried egg perched on top offers the perfect contrast to the heartier ingredients.

—CAMILA CHAPARRO, *Test Cook*

'Nduja with Beans and Greens

SERVES 4   TOTAL TIME: 20 MINUTES

6 ounces 'njuda or merguez sausage, casings removed

2 (15-ounce) cans cannellini beans (1 can rinsed, 1 can undrained)

1 pound kale, stemmed and chopped

1 ounce Parmesan cheese, grated (½ cup), divided

4 large eggs

STAPLE INGREDIENTS:

Extra-virgin olive oil
Table salt
Pepper

---

1. Cook 'nduja in Dutch oven over medium-high heat, breaking up meat with wooden spoon, until meat darkens in color and fat renders, 3 to 5 minutes.

2. Stir in beans and their liquid, kale, and ¼ teaspoon pepper and bring to simmer. Reduce heat to medium-low, cover, and cook, stirring occasionally, until kale is tender and sauce has thickened slightly, 5 to 7 minutes. Off heat, stir in ¼ cup Parmesan.

3. Meanwhile, heat 1 tablespoon olive oil in 12-inch nonstick skillet over medium-high heat until shimmering. Add eggs to skillet and sprinkle with ¼ teaspoon salt and ¼ teaspoon pepper. Cover and cook for 1 minute. Remove from heat and let sit for 15 to 45 seconds for runny yolks, 45 to 60 seconds for soft but set yolks, or about 2 minutes for medium-set yolks.

4. Serve beans and kale with fried eggs, sprinkling with remaining ¼ cup Parmesan and drizzling with olive oil to taste.

YOU CAN SERVE WITH
CRUSTY BREAD

There are endless variations of the Korean comfort food kimchi bokkeumbap, but they all showcase kimchi's fermented umami goodness, often using its juices in the sauce. For my take I do just that, rounding it out with sweet and funky gochujang. Leftover rice (arguably the best way to use it up) soaks up the deliciously pungent liquid, and ham steak nuggets add surprise salty, savory bites. My favorite part, though? The crispy bits of rice from the bottom of the pan. Make sure not to peek while it's cooking—let it do its thing undisturbed. Kimchi bokkeumbap is typically made with leftover short-grain white rice, but you can use any rice you have kicking around your fridge (or, see pages 249–251 if you need a fresh batch).

—SAM BLOCK, *Test Cook*

Kimchi and Ham Steak Fried Rice

SERVES 4   TOTAL TIME: 30 MINUTES

1   pound ham steak, cut into ¼-inch pieces

1¼ cups cabbage kimchi, drained with ¼ cup juice reserved, kimchi cut into 1-inch pieces

3   tablespoons gochujang paste or sauce

6   scallions, white and green parts separated and sliced thin on bias

4   cups cooked rice (preferably short-grain)

STAPLE INGREDIENTS:

Vegetable oil
Table Salt
Pepper

1. Heat 2 tablespoons vegetable oil in 12-inch nonstick skillet over medium-high heat until just smoking. Add ham and cook, stirring frequently, until beginning to brown, 6 to 8 minutes. Stir in kimchi and reserved juice, gochujang, scallion whites, 2 tablespoons water, and ¼ teaspoon pepper. Fold in rice until well combined.

2. Firmly press into compact, even layer. Cover and cook, without stirring, until rice begins to crisp, about 2 minutes. Uncover, reduce heat to medium, and continue to cook until bottom of rice is golden brown, 4 to 6 minutes. Season with salt and pepper to taste, sprinkle with scallion greens, and serve.

Fresh
Catch

Smoked paprika is a great spice to keep on hand—it lends that smoky, just-grilled essence while keeping things indoors. Here, it's sprinkled on salmon fillets before cooking, so the spice blooms in the oil and intensifies, and then again over the cooked fish as an extra layer of flavor. While the salmon rests, green beans get spotty brown in the same skillet and then gently steam for a few minutes just before serving (no mushy, overcooked beans here). Pickled banana peppers and a healthy dose of smashed garlic add heat and bright briny kick.

—BRENNA DONOVAN, *Editor*

Pan-Seared Salmon with Smoked Paprika and Spicy Green Beans

SERVES 4   TOTAL TIME: 30 MINUTES

4   (6- to 8-ounce) skin-on salmon fillets, 1 inch thick

1¼ teaspoons smoked paprika, divided

1   pound green beans, trimmed

6   garlic cloves, smashed and peeled

½   cup jarred hot banana pepper rings

STAPLE INGREDIENTS:

Extra-virgin olive oil
Table salt
Pepper

1. Pat salmon dry with paper towels and sprinkle with 1 teaspoon paprika, ½ teaspoon salt, and ¼ teaspoon pepper. Heat 1 teaspoon olive oil in 12-inch nonstick skillet over medium-high heat until just smoking. Place salmon skin side up in skillet and cook until well browned and center is still translucent when checked with tip of paring knife and registers 125 degrees (for medium-rare), 4 to 6 minutes per side. Transfer to serving dish and sprinkle with remaining ¼ teaspoon paprika. Wipe out skillet with paper towels.

2. Heat 1 tablespoon oil in now-empty skillet over medium-high heat until just smoking. Add green beans, garlic, ½ teaspoon salt, and ¼ teaspoon pepper and cook, stirring often, until green beans and garlic turn spotty brown, about 6 minutes. Add 2 tablespoons water, cover, and reduce heat to medium. Cook until green beans are crisp-tender, about 1 minute. Off heat, stir in banana pepper rings and season with salt and pepper to taste. Serve.

YOU CAN SERVE WITH
RICE OR COUSCOUS

Living in New England, I'm ready to dive headfirst into spring at the first sign of the seasons changing. And when I want to be transported to warmer days, I make this ingenious (and subtly elegant) Easter brunch–like meal. The poached salmon couldn't be easier—instead of using a steaming rack, thick asparagus spears serve as a bed to elevate the salmon fillets above the water. When it's ready (less than 10 minutes later), you use that poaching liquid to create a luxuriously delicate white wine–chive butter sauce. I can't think of a better way to celebrate taking my winter boots out of rotation.

—BRENNA DONOVAN, *Editor*

Salmon with Asparagus and Chive Butter Sauce

SERVES 4   TOTAL TIME: 30 MINUTES

1   pound thick asparagus, trimmed

4   (6- to 8-ounce) skinless salmon fillets, 1 inch thick

½   cup dry white wine

2   tablespoons chopped fresh chives

    Lemon wedges

STAPLE INGREDIENTS:

Unsalted butter
Table salt
Pepper

1. Lay asparagus in single layer in 12-inch skillet, then add 1 cup water and ¼ teaspoon salt. Pat salmon dry with paper towels and sprinkle with ½ teaspoon salt and ¼ teaspoon pepper, then lay across asparagus spears in skillet. Bring water to boil over high heat. Reduce heat to medium, cover, and cook until asparagus is tender and salmon is still translucent when checked with tip of paring knife and registers 125 degrees (for medium-rare), about 8 minutes. Transfer salmon and asparagus to platter.

2. Add wine to skillet, increase heat to medium-high, and simmer mixture uncovered for 5 minutes. Off heat, whisk in 3 tablespoons butter and chives and season with salt and pepper to taste. Pour sauce over salmon and asparagus. Serve with lemon wedges.

YOU CAN SERVE WITH
**QUINOA, RICE,
COUSCOUS, OR
CRUSTY BREAD**

A one-pan dish is always a winner in my busy house because it means fewer dishes after the kids go to bed. Combine low-prep, buttery salmon and some quick-cooking veggies on a baking sheet and you have a weeknight favorite. Roasted in a hot oven, the fish cooks through to a silky medium-rare while the intense heat tames the bitterness of the broccoli rabe and crisps up its leaves for a crunchy textural contrast—all in under 15 minutes. To bring the dish together, a nutty, lemony gremolata topping hits it out of the park.

—RUSSELL SELANDER, *Test Cook*

Roasted Salmon and Broccoli Rabe with Pistachio Gremolata

SERVES 4   TOTAL TIME: 25 MINUTES

¼   cup shelled pistachios, toasted and chopped fine

2   tablespoons minced fresh parsley

1   teaspoon grated lemon zest, plus lemon wedges for serving

1   pound broccoli rabe, trimmed and cut into 1½-inch lengths

4   (6- to 8-ounce) skinless salmon fillets, 1 inch thick

STAPLE INGREDIENTS:

Extra-virgin olive oil
Table salt
Pepper

1. Adjust oven rack to middle position and heat oven to 450 degrees. Combine pistachios, parsley, and lemon zest in bowl; set gremolata aside until ready to serve.

2. Toss broccoli rabe with 2 tablespoons olive oil, ¼ teaspoon salt, and ¼ teaspoon pepper in bowl. Arrange on half of rimmed baking sheet. Pat salmon dry with paper towels, rub with 2 teaspoons oil, and sprinkle with ½ teaspoon salt and ¼ teaspoon pepper. Arrange salmon skinned side down on empty half of sheet.

3. Roast until centers of salmon are still translucent when checked with tip of paring knife and register 125 degrees (for medium-rare) and broccoli rabe is tender, 8 to 12 minutes. Sprinkle salmon with reserved gremolata and serve with lemon wedges.

Seasoned rice vinegar is a fantastic ingredient to keep in your cupboard for creating dipping sauces or marinades with a little extra *oomph*—the added sugar and salt bring more nuance to a dish than regular rice vinegar. Here, it perks up sticky, tender sushi rice and also gets whisked with nutty sesame oil to coat crunchy, fresh cucumbers that serve as the perfect contrast to rich and fatty salmon.

—BRENNA DONOVAN, *Editor*

Salmon and Rice with Cucumber Salad

SERVES 4   TOTAL TIME: 50 MINUTES

1   cup sushi rice, rinsed

¼   cup seasoned rice vinegar, divided

4   (6- to 8-ounce) skin-on salmon fillets, 1 inch thick

1   English cucumber, halved lengthwise and sliced thin crosswise

1   tablespoon toasted sesame oil

STAPLE INGREDIENTS:

Vegetable oil
Table salt
Pepper

1. Bring rice, 1½ cups water, and ½ teaspoon salt to boil in small saucepan over high heat. Reduce heat to maintain bare simmer, cover, and cook until water is absorbed, about 20 minutes.

2. Remove pot from heat and let sit, covered, until rice is tender, about 10 minutes. Drizzle rice with 1 tablespoon vinegar, fluff with fork, season with salt and pepper to taste, then cover to keep warm and set aside.

3. Meanwhile, pat salmon dry with paper towels and sprinkle with ½ teaspoon salt and ¼ teaspoon pepper. Heat 1 teaspoon vegetable oil in 12-inch nonstick skillet over medium-high heat until just smoking. Place salmon skin side up in skillet and cook until well browned and centers are still translucent when checked with tip of paring knife and register 125 degrees (for medium-rare), 4 to 6 minutes per side; remove from heat.

4. Toss cucumber with sesame oil, remaining 3 tablespoons vinegar, and ¼ teaspoon salt together in bowl then season with salt and pepper to taste. Serve with salmon and rice.

YOU CAN SERVE WITH
**CRUSTY BREAD OR
A SIMPLE SALAD**

The juices that result from cooking a packet of fish, tomatoes, and lemon are the highlight of this meal (besides the crispy potatoes, of course). For such a simple combination, this dish is surprisingly fragrant, and you'll be glad for those potatoes to soak up all the juices. Depending on the size of your lemon, you may have a little left over—save it for another use or spritz it over the cooked fish for an acidic kick.

—STEPHANIE PIXLEY, *Editor*

Lemon-Poached Halibut Packets with Roasted Fingerling Potatoes

SERVES 4   **TOTAL TIME: 45 MINUTES**

1½   pounds fingerling potatoes, halved lengthwise

8   ounces grape or cherry tomatoes, halved

4   (6- to 8-ounce) skinless halibut, mahi-mahi, red snapper, striped bass, or swordfish fillets, 1 inch thick

8   thin lemon slices

2   tablespoons minced fresh basil, chives, or parsley

STAPLE INGREDIENTS:

Extra-virgin olive oil
Table salt
Pepper

1. Adjust oven rack to lower-middle position and heat oven to 450 degrees. Toss potatoes with 2 teaspoons olive oil, ½ teaspoon salt, and ½ teaspoon pepper in bowl, then arrange cut side down in single layer on rimmed baking sheet. Roast until cut sides begin to brown, about 10 minutes.

2. Meanwhile, lay four 12-inch-long pieces of aluminum foil on counter. Place one-quarter of tomatoes in center of each piece of foil, then place 1 fillet on each tomato pile. Sprinkle each fillet with ⅛ teaspoon salt and pinch pepper, then top with 2 lemon slices and drizzle with 1 teaspoon oil. Pull edges of foil up around fish and tomatoes and crimp to form packet.

3. Place packets on top of potatoes on sheet and bake until halibut registers 130 degrees, 15 to 18 minutes (insert an instant-read thermometer through the foil into thickest part of fish to test for doneness). Carefully open packets, allowing steam to escape away from you, then let halibut rest in packets for 10 minutes.

4. Divide potatoes among 4 bowls. Using thin metal spatula, gently slide fish and tomatoes onto potatoes and pour accumulated juices over top. Sprinkle with basil and serve.

A squeeze of lemon is the quintessential pairing for fish, and in this recipe a miso-lemon marinade takes that pairing to new heights. The mixture gets rubbed over sea bass to infuse the fillets with savory, citrusy flavor. While the fish marinates, meaty mushrooms and hearty kale roast and get slightly crispy in the oven. After stirring the vegetables to ensure even cooking, the fish goes on top and it all gets popped back into the oven, where the funky-sweet miso and lemon permeate the vegetables.

—BRENNA DONOVAN, *Editor*

Sheet-Pan Miso Sea Bass with Kale and Mushrooms

SERVES 4   TOTAL TIME: 35 MINUTES

⅓ cup white miso

1 teaspoon grated lemon zest plus 2 tablespoons juice (2 lemons), plus lemon wedges for serving

4 (6- to 8-ounce) skin-on black sea bass or red snapper fillets, or skinless halibut fillets, 1 inch thick

1 pound kale, stemmed and chopped

1 pound shiitake mushrooms, stemmed and sliced ½ inch thick

STAPLE INGREDIENTS:

Extra-virgin olive oil
Table salt
Pepper

1. Adjust oven rack to lower-middle position and heat oven to 450 degrees. Whisk miso, 2 tablespoons olive oil, and lemon zest and juice together in bowl. Rub sea bass all over with miso-lemon paste; set aside.

2. Vigorously squeeze and massage kale with hands in large bowl until leaves are uniformly darkened and slightly wilted, about 1 minute. Add mushrooms, ¼ cup oil, ½ teaspoon salt, and ¼ teaspoon pepper and toss to combine. Spread vegetables in single layer on rimmed baking sheet and roast until liquid from mushrooms has mostly evaporated and kale is beginning to crisp on edges, 8 to 12 minutes.

3. Remove sheet from oven, stir vegetables, and redistribute into single layer. Place reserved fish, skin (or skinned) side down, on vegetables. Roast until sea bass is opaque and registers 135 degrees, 12 to 15 minutes. Serve sea bass and vegetables with lemon wedges.

YOU CAN SERVE WITH

CRUSTY BREAD, RICE, OR QUINOA

Tilapia has a whole lot going for it: It's inexpensive, easy to find, and freezes wonderfully so you can pull it out for a fancier-than-it-feels meal any night of the week. The trick to even browning and precise cooking is to split the fillets down their natural seams into thick and thin portions and cook them separately. I made a bright, rich orange-tarragon compound butter to melt over the tilapia and blistered green beans, creating a decadent, silky sauce that even my pickiest eater enjoys (butter solves everything). Salty smoked almonds mixed into the beans add pleasant smokiness and crunch.

—RUSSELL SELANDER, *Test Cook*

Orange-Tarragon Tilapia with Smoky Green Beans

SERVES 4   TOTAL TIME: 35 MINUTES

¼ cup minced fresh tarragon

1 teaspoon grated orange zest

4 (6- to 8-ounce) skinless tilapia, catfish, flounder, or sole fillets, halved lengthwise down natural seam

1 pound green beans, trimmed

½ cup smoked almonds, chopped fine

STAPLE INGREDIENTS:

Unsalted butter
Table salt
Pepper

1. Soften 3 tablespoons butter, then mash with tarragon, orange zest, ¼ teaspoon salt, and ⅛ teaspoon pepper in bowl with fork until combined; set tarragon butter aside. Meanwhile, sprinkle tilapia with ½ teaspoon salt and let sit at room temperature for 15 minutes.

2. Combine green beans, ¼ cup water, additional 1 tablespoon unsalted butter, ¼ teaspoon salt, and ¼ teaspoon pepper in 12-inch nonstick skillet. Cover and cook over medium-high heat, shaking pan occasionally, until water has evaporated, 6 to 8 minutes. Uncover and continue to cook until green beans are blistered and browned, about 2 minutes longer. Add 1 tablespoon reserved tarragon butter and smoked almonds and toss to combine. Season with salt and pepper to taste then transfer to serving platter and tent with aluminum foil to keep warm.

3. Pat tilapia dry with paper towels. Melt additional 1 tablespoon unsalted butter in now-empty skillet over medium-high heat. Add thick halves of fillets to skillet and cook until tilapia is golden brown on both sides, 2 to 3 minutes per side; transfer to platter with green beans.

4. Melt additional 1 tablespoon unsalted butter in again-empty skillet over medium-high heat. Add thin halves of fillets and cook until golden brown on both sides, about 1 minute per side; transfer to platter with green beans. Top fillets with remaining reserved tarragon butter and serve.

YOU CAN SERVE WITH
A SIMPLE SALAD

My favorite neighborhood restaurant makes the best roasted cod with potatoes, and when I want to re-create it at home I turn to this recipe. Start by microwaving sliced potatoes with a little garlic and oil to give them a head start, then shingle them into individual piles on a baking sheet. Place a piece of cod on each pile and top with butter, thyme sprigs, and slices of lemon. The seasonings gently baste the cod as it roasts, drawing the herbal and citrus flavors through the fillets and down over the potatoes. It's unexpected comfort food at its finest.

—BRENNA DONOVAN, *Editor*

Lemon-Herb Roasted Cod with Crispy Garlic Potatoes

SERVES 4   TOTAL TIME: 45 MINUTES

1½ pounds russet potatoes, unpeeled, sliced into ¼-inch-thick rounds

3 garlic cloves, minced

4 (6- to 8-ounce) skinless cod, black sea bass, haddock, hake, or pollack fillets, 1 inch thick

4 sprigs fresh thyme

4 thin lemon slices

STAPLE INGREDIENTS:

Extra-virgin olive oil
Unsalted butter
Table salt
Pepper

1. Cut 3 tablespoons butter into ¼-inch pieces and set aside. Adjust oven rack to lower-middle position and heat oven to 425 degrees. Brush rimmed baking sheet with 1 tablespoon olive oil. Toss potatoes with garlic, 2 tablespoons oil, ¼ teaspoon salt, and ¼ teaspoon pepper in bowl. Microwave until potatoes are just tender, 12 to 14 minutes, stirring once halfway through.

2. Shingle potatoes on prepared sheet, making 4 rectangular piles that measure roughly 4 by 6 inches. Pat cod dry with paper towels, sprinkle with ½ teaspoon salt and ¼ teaspoon pepper, and place 1 fillet skinned side down on each potato pile. Arrange butter pieces, thyme sprigs, and lemon slices on top of cod.

3. Roast until fish flakes apart when gently prodded with paring knife and registers 135 degrees, 15 to 18 minutes. Slide spatula underneath potatoes and cod, gently transfer to individual plates, and serve.

Radishes are one of my favorite things to roast. Yes, they're often served raw on top of a salad, or pickled and added to a taco, but the real magic happens when you cook them, transforming their peppery crunchiness into savory deliciousness. As for the cauliflower, I toss wedges and halved radishes with garlic, butter, and lemon zest, then use a steam-then-roast method to cook them (all in the oven): I start by cooking them covered on a sheet pan, then take the aluminum foil off halfway through so the cauliflower caramelizes. I serve it all with flaky cod fillets sprinkled with radish greens as a no-waste garnish.

—RUSSELL SELANDER, *Test Cook*

Sautéed Cod with Roasted Cauliflower and Radishes

SERVES 4   TOTAL TIME: 40 MINUTES

1   head cauliflower (2 pounds), trimmed and cut through core into 8 wedges

12   ounces radishes with their greens, radishes trimmed and halved, 2 tablespoons radish greens minced

6   garlic cloves, minced

1   teaspoon grated lemon zest plus 1 tablespoon juice

4   (6- to 8-ounce) skinless cod, black sea bass, haddock, hake, or pollack fillets, 1 inch thick

STAPLE INGREDIENTS:

Extra-virgin olive oil
Table salt
Pepper

1. Adjust oven racks to lowest and middle positions and heat oven to 450 degrees. Toss cauliflower with radishes, garlic, lemon zest, ¼ cup olive oil, ½ teaspoon salt, and ¼ teaspoon pepper in large bowl, then transfer to aluminum foil–lined rimmed baking sheet. Arrange cauliflower wedges cut side down, cover sheet tightly with aluminum foil, and roast on lower rack for 10 minutes.

2. Remove foil and continue to roast until bottoms of cauliflower wedges are golden, 10 to 15 minutes. Remove sheet from oven and, using spatula, gently flip cauliflower wedges. Return sheet to oven and roast until radishes are tender and cauliflower is golden all over, 10 to 15 minutes. Remove from oven and season with salt and pepper to taste.

3. Meanwhile, pat cod dry with paper towels and sprinkle with ½ teaspoon salt and ¼ teaspoon pepper. Heat 1 tablespoon oil in 12-inch ovensafe nonstick skillet over medium-high heat until just smoking. Lay fillets in skillet and, using spatula, lightly press fillets for 20 to 30 seconds to ensure even contact with skillet. Cook until golden brown on first side, 1 to 2 minutes.

4. Using 2 spatulas, flip fillets, then transfer skillet to upper rack in oven. Roast until fish flakes apart when gently prodded with paring knife and registers 135 degrees, 7 to 10 minutes. Serve cod and vegetables immediately, sprinkling vegetables with radish greens.

YOU CAN SERVE WITH
A SIMPLE SALAD

Inspired by arroz verde, I like to toss still-warm white rice with a garlic and cilantro vinaigrette so it drinks up all of the sauce's tart, herbal flavors. For this recipe, it's critical to have uniform grains of rice, so I cook it like pasta—dump the rice into a pot of boiling water (no need for finicky ratios!) and drain it when it's done. While all that is happening, sear cod fillets in a piping-hot skillet to achieve a gorgeous crust before gently finishing them in the oven. Once everything is ready, drizzle some of the reserved cilantro sauce over the top to tie it all together.

—RUSSELL SELANDER, *Test Cook*

Cod with Cilantro Rice

SERVES 4   TOTAL TIME: 30 MINUTES

3   cups fresh cilantro leaves and stems, chopped coarse

2   tablespoons red wine vinegar

2   garlic cloves, smashed and peeled

1   cup long-grain white rice

4   (6- to 8-ounce) skinless cod, black sea bass, haddock, hake, or pollack fillets, 1 inch thick

STAPLE INGREDIENTS:

Extra-virgin olive oil
Table salt
Pepper

1. Adjust oven rack to middle position and heat oven to 425 degrees. Pulse cilantro, vinegar, garlic, ¼ teaspoon salt, and ¼ teaspoon pepper in food processor until finely chopped, about 12 pulses, scraping down sides of bowl as needed. Transfer to bowl, whisk in ½ cup olive oil, and set aside.

2. Bring 2 quarts water to boil in large saucepan. Stir in rice and 1 teaspoon salt and cook until rice is tender, about 12 minutes. Drain rice well, return to saucepan, and stir in ¼ cup reserved cilantro sauce; season with salt and pepper to taste. Cover and set aside until ready to serve.

3. Meanwhile, pat cod dry with paper towels and sprinkle with ½ teaspoon salt and ¼ teaspoon pepper. Heat 1 tablespoon oil in 12-inch ovensafe nonstick skillet over medium-high heat until just smoking. Lay fillets in skillet and, using spatula, lightly press fillets for 20 to 30 seconds to ensure even contact with skillet. Cook until golden brown on first side, 1 to 2 minutes.

4. Using 2 spatulas, flip fillets, then transfer skillet to oven. Roast until fish flakes apart when gently prodded with paring knife and registers 135 degrees, 7 to 10 minutes. Transfer cod to platter, drizzle with remaining reserved cilantro sauce, and serve with reserved rice.

If something is sesame-crusted, I'm on board—it delivers the same crunch as a bread crumb coating, but takes it up a notch. Here the seeds serve two purposes: They get nutty and crispy, delivering little pops of flavor with every bite, and they also shield the easy-to-overcook tuna from the heat so it stays rare in the center. Stir-fried bok choy and ginger is the perfect pairing for the melt-in-your-mouth steaks, and bright, umami-rich ponzu adds aromatic depth.

—BRENNA DONOVAN, *Editor*

Sesame-Crusted Tuna with Gingery Bok Choy

SERVE 4   TOTAL TIME: 30 MINUTES

4   (6- to 8-ounce) skinless tuna steaks, 1 inch thick

¾   cup sesame seeds

6   heads baby bok choy (4 ounces each), stalks halved crosswise, greens chopped coarse

1   tablespoon grated fresh ginger

3   tablespoons ponzu sauce

STAPLE INGREDIENTS:

Vegetable oil
Table salt
Pepper

1. Pat tuna dry with paper towels then rub all over with 1 tablespoon vegetable oil and sprinkle with ½ teaspoon salt and ¼ teaspoon pepper. Place sesame seeds on plate and, working with one steak at a time, press both sides firmly into seeds to coat evenly.

2. Heat 2 tablespoons oil in 12-inch nonstick skillet over medium-high heat until just smoking. Add steaks and cook, flipping every 1 to 2 minutes, until opaque at perimeter and center is translucent red when checked with tip of paring knife and registers 110 degrees (for rare), 2 to 4 minutes. Transfer steaks to cutting board and set aside while cooking bok choy.

3. Wipe skillet clean with paper towels and heat 2 tablespoons oil over medium-high heat until just smoking. Add bok choy stalks and ½ teaspoon salt and cook, without stirring, until beginning to brown, about 5 minutes.

4. Push stalks to sides of skillet, add ginger and 1 teaspoon oil, and cook, stirring constantly until fragrant, about 20 seconds. Stir in bok choy greens and ponzu sauce and cook, stirring constantly, until greens are wilted, about 1 minute; remove from heat. Slice tuna ¼ inch thick and serve with bok choy.

YOU CAN SERVE WITH

**RICE, QUINOA,
OR COUSCOUS**

YOU CAN SERVE WITH
**CRUSTY BREAD OR
A SIMPLE SALAD**

Scallops are hands-down one of my favorite seafoods: I call them the filet mignon of the sea. But as fancy as they seem, they're dead-simple to cook. The secret to perfect scallops is twofold: getting a gorgeous crust, and adding flavors that accentuate their sweetness. For the crust, making sure the scallops are room temperature and dry to the touch is key before searing them in a hot pan. For the flavors, I pair the seared scallops with mashed butternut squash and a sage browned butter to balance the sweetness with a potent herby zing.

—RUSSELL SELANDER, *Test Cook*

Seared Scallops with Squash and Sage Butter

SERVES 4   TOTAL TIME: 30 MINUTES

1½   pounds large sea scallops, tendons removed

2   pounds butternut squash, peeled, seeded, and cut into 1-inch pieces (5½ cups)

1   tablespoon chopped fresh sage

1   tablespoon lemon juice

STAPLE INGREDIENTS:

Unsalted butter
Table salt
Pepper

1. Place scallops on large plate lined with triple layer of paper towels. Top with paper towels and press gently on scallops to dry. Let scallops sit at room temperature for 10 minutes. Meanwhile, microwave squash in covered bowl until tender, 8 to 12 minutes, stirring halfway through. Drain, if necessary, then add 1 tablespoon butter and ½ teaspoon salt and mash with potato masher in large bowl until smooth and well combined. Cover and keep warm until ready to serve.

2. Sprinkle scallops with ½ teaspoon salt and ¼ teaspoon pepper. Melt 1 tablespoon butter in 12-inch nonstick skillet over medium-high heat. Add half of scallops in single layer, flat side down, and cook until well browned, 1½ to 2 minutes. Flip scallops and cook until sides are firm and centers are opaque, 30 to 90 seconds (remove smaller scallops as they finish cooking). Transfer to plate and tent with aluminum foil. Wipe out skillet with paper towels and repeat with 1 tablespoon butter and remaining scallops.

3. Melt 3 tablespoons butter in now-empty skillet over medium heat. Continue to cook, swirling skillet constantly, until butter begins to brown and has nutty aroma, 1 to 2 minutes. Add sage and cook until fragrant, about 1 minute. Off heat, stir in lemon juice. Pour sauce over scallops and serve with squash puree.

YOU CAN SERVE WITH

**CRUSTY BREAD OR
A SIMPLE SALAD**

Peeling your own shrimp might sound like a tedious task, but it's well worth it—once you save the shells to make shrimp stock you'll never look back. The briny, savory elixir adds depth to an otherwise simple risotto that is even simpler to prepare. (No endless stirring required!) A final flourish of a buttery adobo sauce spices things up. For fat, juicy chunks of shrimp, use extra-large shrimp (21 to 25 per pound). Some shrimp are treated with salt or additives like sodium tripolyphosphate (STPP); if using treated shrimp, skip adding salt to the shrimp in step 1.

—RUSSELL SELANDER, *Test Cook*

Chipotle Shrimp Risotto

SERVES 4   TOTAL TIME: 55 MINUTES

1 pound shrimp, peeled, deveined, cut into thirds, and shells reserved

1 onion, chopped fine

6 garlic cloves, minced

1½ cups Arborio rice

1 teaspoon minced canned chipotle chile in adobo sauce, plus 3 tablespoons adobo sauce

STAPLE INGREDIENTS:

Extra-virgin olive oil
Unsalted butter
Table salt
Pepper

1. Toss shrimp with ½ teaspoon salt in bowl; set aside. Heat 1 tablespoon olive oil in large saucepan over high heat until shimmering. Add shrimp shells and cook, stirring frequently, until spotty brown, 2 to 4 minutes. Carefully add 5½ cups water and ½ teaspoon salt, scraping up any browned bits, and bring to boil. Reduce heat to low and simmer for 5 minutes. Strain stock through fine-mesh strainer set over large bowl, pressing on solids to extract as much liquid as possible; discard solids. Return stock to now-empty pot, cover, and maintain gentle simmer over low heat until ready to use.

2. Melt 3 tablespoons butter in Dutch oven over medium heat. Add onion and cook, stirring frequently, until softened, about 5 minutes. Stir in garlic and cook until fragrant, about 30 seconds. Stir in rice and cook, stirring frequently, until grains are translucent around edges, about 3 minutes. Stir 4 cups hot stock into rice mixture then reduce heat to medium-low, cover, and simmer until almost all liquid has been absorbed and rice is just al dente, 16 to 19 minutes, stirring twice during simmering.

3. Add 1 cup hot stock to risotto and stir gently and constantly until risotto becomes creamy, about 3 minutes. Stir in shrimp, cover pot, and let sit off heat until shrimp are just opaque, about 5 minutes. Adjust consistency with remaining hot stock as needed and season with salt and pepper to taste.

4. Microwave 3 tablespoons butter, chipotle, and adobo sauce in small bowl at 10-second intervals until butter is melted and fragrant. Serve risotto with chipotle butter.

This recipe is the perfect answer to when I want something light and healthful, but still hearty enough to feel like a meal. Nutty, chewy barley pairs wonderfully with shrimp and crunchy-tart apple, but marinated feta is the star of the show here: The tangy cheese and its herby oil are turned into a dressing for the barley to ensure all that goodness gets dispersed throughout the whole salad. I like to use extra-large shrimp (21 to 25 per pound). Some shrimp are treated with salt or additives like sodium tripolyphosphate (STPP); if using treated shrimp, skip adding salt to the shrimp in step 2.

—BRENNA DONOVAN, *Editor*

Shrimp with Warm Barley Salad

SERVES 4   TOTAL TIME: 35 MINUTES

1   cup quick-cooking barley

1½ pounds shrimp, peeled and deveined

¼   cup cider vinegar

4   ounces marinated feta, crumbled (1 cup), plus ¼ cup marinated feta oil

1   apple, cored, halved, and sliced thin

STAPLE INGREDIENTS:

Extra-virgin olive oil
Table salt
Pepper

1. Bring 1½ cups water and ¼ teaspoon salt to boil in medium saucepan over high heat. Add barley, cover, reduce heat to low, and cook until tender and most of water is absorbed, about 10 minutes. Spread onto rimmed baking sheet to cool.

2. Meanwhile, pat shrimp dry with paper towels and sprinkle with ¼ teaspoon salt and ¼ teaspoon pepper. Heat 2 tablespoons olive oil in 12-inch nonstick skillet over medium-high heat until just smoking. Add shrimp and cook, stirring occasionally, until opaque throughout, 3 to 6 minutes.

3. Whisk vinegar, feta oil, ¾ teaspoon pepper, and ½ teaspoon salt together in large bowl. Add barley, apple, and feta and toss to coat. Season with salt and pepper to taste and top with shrimp. Serve.

I used to think mussels were best eaten in a restaurant, but since I've discovered this recipe I'm a true mussels-at-home convert. Spicy, savory chorizo is browned in a Dutch oven first, then that tasty fond gets scraped up with the help of a can of crushed tomatoes. Toss in the mussels, cover, and stir every so often until they pop open. In the meantime, toast up thick slices of hearty bread and rub with garlic when they're still warm: perfect for dipping into the delicious broth. Before cooking, discard any mussel with an unpleasant odor, a cracked or broken shell, or a shell that won't close.

—BRENNA DONOVAN, *Editor*

Mussels, Chorizo, and Tomatoes with Garlic Toasts

SERVES 4   TOTAL TIME: 30 MINUTES

12 ounces Spanish-style chorizo sausage, cut into ½-inch pieces

4 garlic cloves (3 minced, 1 peeled)

1 (28-ounce) can crushed tomatoes

4 pounds mussels, scrubbed and debearded

8 (1-inch-thick) slices rustic bread

STAPLE INGREDIENTS:

Extra-virgin olive oil
Table salt

1. Adjust oven rack 6 inches from broiler element and heat broiler. Cook chorizo in 3 tablespoons olive oil in large Dutch oven over medium heat, stirring occasionally, until chorizo is browned, 5 to 7 minutes. Stir in minced garlic and cook until fragrant, about 30 seconds. Stir in tomatoes and ½ teaspoon salt, bring to simmer, and cook until flavors meld, about 3 minutes. Increase heat to high and stir in mussels. Cover and cook, stirring occasionally, until mussels open, 3 to 7 minutes. Discard any unopened mussels.

2. Place bread on aluminum foil–lined rimmed baking sheet and broil until deep golden on both sides, 1 to 2 minutes per side. While toast is still warm, lightly rub 1 side of each toast with peeled garlic and drizzle with olive oil to taste. Serve mussels with garlic toast.

YOU CAN SERVE WITH
A SIMPLE SALAD

Noodle Night

Broccoli rabe and pasta is a classic combination that's often paired with sausage—a delicious dish that I find no fault with, but which I modified here with chicken. I love this version for two reasons. One, I can use store-bought rotisserie chicken if I don't feel like cooking it myself (see page 253 for a recipe for poached chicken if you're not like me); and two, roasted garlic. My favorite trick for peeling a whopping 16 (!) cloves of garlic? Remove the outer papery skin of a garlic head, place it in a 2-cup wide-mouth Mason jar, screw on the lid, and shake until the skins come off.

—STEPHANIE PIXLEY, *Editor*

Orecchiette with Roasted Garlic, Broccoli Rabe, and Chicken

SERVES 4 TO 6   TOTAL TIME: 35 MINUTES

16   garlic cloves, peeled

2   cups shredded cooked chicken

1   pound broccoli rabe, trimmed and cut into 1½-inch lengths

1   pound orecchiette or medium shells

2   ounces Parmesan cheese, grated (1 cup), plus extra for serving

STAPLE INGREDIENTS:

Extra-virgin olive oil
Table salt
Pepper

1. Adjust oven rack to upper-middle position and heat oven to 425 degrees. Combine garlic, ⅓ cup olive oil, ½ teaspoon salt, and ½ teaspoon pepper in 8-inch square baking dish and cover with aluminum foil. Bake, stirring occasionally, until garlic is caramelized and soft, about 20 minutes. Let cool slightly, then mash garlic and oil into paste with fork. Stir in cooked chicken.

2. Meanwhile, bring 4 quarts water to boil in large pot. Add broccoli rabe and 1 tablespoon salt and cook until crisp-tender, 1 to 3 minutes; transfer to paper towel–lined plate. Return pot of water to boil, add pasta, and cook, stirring often, until al dente. Reserve ½ cup cooking water, then drain pasta and return it to pot.

3. Add chicken-garlic mixture, broccoli rabe, and Parmesan to pasta in pot and toss to combine. Adjust consistency with reserved cooking water as needed and season with salt and pepper to taste. Serve, passing extra Parmesan separately.

Because it's a fast, satisfying, and flavorful weeknight dinner that everyone in my family will eat (and that lends itself to lots of improvisation), this recipe is quickly becoming our go-to favorite. Savory soy sauce serves as a marinade for the chicken as well as the backbone for a stir-fry sauce kicked up a notch with chili-garlic sauce. Quick-cooking bok choy brings freshness and contrasting crunch to chewy, hearty Chinese egg noodles, but feel free to experiment with substituting your favorite veg instead.

—CAMILA CHAPARRO, *Test Cook*

Chicken Lo Mein with Bok Choy

SERVES 4   TOTAL TIME: 35 MINUTES

1 pound boneless skinless chicken breasts, trimmed and sliced crosswise ¼ inch thick

¼ cup soy sauce, divided

12 ounces fresh Chinese noodles or 8 ounces dried Chinese noodles

1 pound baby bok choy, halved lengthwise and sliced crosswise ½ inch thick

1 tablespoon Asian chili-garlic sauce

STAPLE INGREDIENT:

Vegetable oil

1. Toss chicken with 1 tablespoon soy sauce in bowl; set aside while cooking noodles. Bring 4 quarts water to boil in large pot. Add noodles and cook, stirring often, until tender. Drain noodles and rinse thoroughly with cold water; set aside.

2. Heat 1 tablespoon vegetable oil in 12-inch nonstick skillet over medium-high heat until just smoking. Add chicken and cook until no longer pink, about 3 minutes. Transfer chicken to large serving bowl. Add 1 tablespoon oil to now-empty skillet and heat over medium-high heat until just smoking. Add bok choy and cook until beginning to soften and char in spots, 2 to 4 minutes. Transfer to bowl with chicken.

3. Add 1 tablespoon oil to again-empty skillet and heat over medium-high heat until just smoking. Add noodles, remaining 3 tablespoons soy sauce, and chili-garlic sauce and toss to combine. Cook until noodles are warmed through, 1 to 2 minutes. Transfer noodles to bowl with chicken and bok choy and toss to combine. Serve.

During the bleak winter months here in the Northeast, I often gravitate to beef stroganoff and other creamy, meat-heavy noodle dishes for a quick hit of coziness. For this version, I brown ground pork with some mushrooms before stirring in broth and scraping up all the savory bits. Cooking the noodles in this saucy mix ensures that they are deeply flavorful from the inside out. Just at the end, I stir in Boursin cheese, delivering quintessential creaminess and complex herby flavor from one ingredient. Even better: There's not a bunch of herbs wasting away in my fridge before I get the chance to use them up.

—LEAH COLINS, *Test Cook*

Creamy Egg Noodles with Pork

SERVES 4   TOTAL TIME: 45 MINUTES

1   pound ground pork

8   ounces cremini or white mushrooms, trimmed and sliced thin

4   cups chicken broth

8   ounces wide egg noodles (4 cups)

1   (5.2-ounce) package Boursin Garlic & Fine Herbs cheese, crumbled (1 cup)

STAPLE INGREDIENTS:

Vegetable oil
Table salt
Pepper

1. Heat 1 tablespoon vegetable oil in Dutch oven over medium-high heat until just smoking. Add pork, mushrooms, and ½ teaspoon salt and cook until liquid has evaporated and pork is beginning to brown, 10 to 12 minutes.

2. Stir in broth, scraping up any browned bits and bring to simmer. Stir in noodles, cover, and cook, stirring occasionally, until noodles are tender, 10 to 12 minutes.

3. Off heat, stir in Boursin until well combined, then let sit for 5 minutes to thicken. (If sauce doesn't thicken after 5 minutes, let sit for additional 5 minutes.) Stir to recombine, season with salt and pepper to taste, and serve.

This veggie-heavy take on pasta alla gricia—the tasty Roman pasta dish made with just pancetta (or traditional guanciale), Pecorino Romano, and lots of black pepper—always hits the spot. The cheese and salty cured meat feel so decadent, but the sweet, meaty roasted red peppers and silky Swiss chard are the perfect foil to the richness. The real secret to the sauce here is the starchy pasta water—it's why the pasta cooks in less water. And if you're used to a heavy-handed pour of salt before you drop the pasta, hold off here—the pancetta adds plenty of saltiness.

—BRENNA DONOVAN, *Editor*

Rigatoni with Swiss Chard, Bell Peppers, and Pancetta

SERVES 4 TO 6   TOTAL TIME: 35 MINUTES

8   ounces pancetta, cut into ¼-inch pieces

1   pound rigatoni or penne

8   ounces Swiss chard, stemmed and cut into ¼-inch-wide strips

2   ounces Pecorino Romano cheese, grated (1 cup), plus extra for serving

1   cup jarred roasted red peppers, rinsed, patted dry and cut into ¼-inch-wide strips

STAPLE INGREDIENTS:

Extra-virgin olive oil
Table Salt
Pepper

1. Heat pancetta and 1 tablespoon olive oil in large Dutch oven over medium-low heat, stirring frequently, until fat is rendered and pancetta is deep golden brown, 12 to 15 minutes. Using slotted spoon, transfer pancetta to bowl; set aside. Pour fat from pot into liquid measuring cup. You should have ¼ to ⅓ cup fat; if you don't have enough, add oil to equal ¼ cup. Return fat to Dutch oven.

2. Meanwhile, bring 2 quarts water to boil in large pot. Add pasta and cook, stirring often, until al dente. Reserve 3 cups cooking water, then drain pasta and return it to pot.

3. Add 1 teaspoon pepper and 2 cups reserved cooking water to reserved fat in Dutch oven and bring to boil over high heat. Boil mixture rapidly, scraping up any browned bits, until reduced to 1½ cups, about 5 minutes. (If you've reduced too far, add more reserved cooking water to equal 1½ cups.) Reduce heat to medium, stir in chard, and simmer until chard begins to wilt, 1 to 3 minutes. Add Pecorino, red peppers, pasta, and pancetta, stirring until cheese is melted and sauce is slightly thickened, about 1 minute.

4. Adjust consistency with remaining reserved cooking water as needed and season with salt and pepper to taste. Serve immediately, passing pepper and extra Pecorino separately.

Dried tortellini are a mainstay in my pantry—they're great for a last-minute meal to whip up when I'm overdue for a grocery trip (which happens a lot, admittedly). Everything takes place in one skillet—after browning some sausage, the tortellini go directly into the same pan with some water. This not only keeps dish duty manageable, but it also keeps the tortellini from bursting open as they often do in vigorously boiling water. Once the pasta is tender, cherry tomatoes join the party and soften into a makeshift sauce. A shower of fresh basil makes this pantry meal feel a little fresher and more aromatic.

—BRENNA DONOVAN, *Editor*

Skillet Tortellini with Sausage and Cherry Tomatoes

SERVES 4   TOTAL TIME: 35 MINUTES

1   **pound sweet or hot Italian sausage, casings removed**

2   **garlic cloves, sliced thin**

12 **ounces dried cheese tortellini**

8   **ounces cherry or grape tomatoes, halved**

2   **tablespoons chopped fresh basil**

STAPLE INGREDIENTS:

Extra-virgin olive oil
Table salt
Pepper

1. Heat 1 tablespoon olive oil in 12-inch nonstick skillet over medium heat until shimmering. Add sausage and cook, breaking up meat with wooden spoon, until no longer pink, about 4 minutes.

2. Add garlic and cook until fragrant, about 30 seconds. Add 4 cups water, pasta, and ¼ teaspoon salt and bring to boil. Reduce heat to medium and simmer, stirring occasionally, until pasta is tender, about 15 minutes.

3. Stir in tomatoes and cook until slightly softened, about 2 minutes. Season with salt and pepper to taste, drizzle with olive oil to taste, and sprinkle with basil. Serve.

'Nduja is a spicy, pork-based, so-soft-it's-spreadable sausage that has its roots in the Calabria region of Italy. Named for its resemblance to French andouille, it's liberally spiced to a fiery brick red and slow-fermented so it takes on a notable tangy funk. Here it melts into crushed tomatoes, quickly simmering away into a supersavory sauce (and because 'nduja is already cooked, this step just takes a minute!). Bright, peppery arugula gets tossed with the sauce and pasta for a little fresh contrast, and then each plate gets topped with more fresh arugula and shaved Pecorino Romano for some dramatic height and a crisp finish.

—CARMEN DONGO, *Test Cook*

Pasta with 'Nduja Tomato Sauce

SERVES 4 TO 6   TOTAL TIME: 30 MINUTES

1   **pound penne or rigatoni**

1   **(14.5-ounce) can crushed tomatoes**

6   **ounces 'njuda sausage, casings removed**

1   **ounce Pecorino Romano cheese, grated (½ cup) plus ½ ounce shaved**

2   **ounces (2 cups) baby arugula, chopped, divided**

STAPLE INGREDIENTS:

Extra-virgin olive oil
Table salt
Pepper

1. Bring 4 quarts water to boil in large pot. Add pasta and 1 tablespoon salt and cook, stirring often, until al dente. Reserve ½ cup cooking water, then drain pasta and return to pot.

2. Meanwhile, bring crushed tomatoes to simmer in large saucepan over medium heat. Cook, stirring occasionally, until thickened slightly, about 10 minutes. Stir in 'nduja, breaking up meat with wooden spoon, and cook until fully incorporated and warmed through, about 1 minute. Season sauce with salt and pepper to taste.

3. Add sauce and grated Pecorino to pasta in pot and toss to coat. Adjust consistency with reserved cooking water as needed and season with salt and pepper to taste. Stir in 1½ cups arugula until just wilted. Just before serving, toss remaining ½ cup arugula with shaved Pecorino and 1 teaspoon olive oil and season with salt and pepper to taste. Top individual portions of pasta with arugula salad. Serve.

VARIATION
Pasta with Sausage Tomato Sauce
Substitute sweet or hot Italian sausage, casings removed, for 'nduja. Before adding crushed tomatoes to saucepan in step 2, heat 1 teaspoon oil over medium heat until shimmering. Add sausage and cook until no longer pink, 3 to 5 minutes.

Chili crisp—a mix of chiles, garlic, and nuts that is deep fried until crunchy and jarred in a spicy, sesame-forward oil—puts all other condiments to shame. It's savory, crunchy, a little spicy, and the perfect companion to whatever you're cooking up: Drizzle it over roasted veggies, scrambled eggs, rice—the list goes on. Here, I use it in a sauce applied to skirt steak before cooking, and as a final flourish to transport the simple steak, charred beans, and noodle dish to a new level of complex yumminess.

—LEAH COLINS, *Test Cook*

Chili-Crisp Steak with Rice Noodles

SERVES 4   TOTAL TIME: 30 MINUTES

12 ounces (⅜-inch-wide) rice noodles

¼ cup chili crisp

2 tablespoons Chinese black vinegar or seasoned rice vinegar

1 pound skirt steak, trimmed and cut with grain into 4 pieces

1 pound green beans, trimmed and halved

STAPLE INGREDIENTS:

Vegetable oil
Table salt
Pepper

1. Pour 2 quarts boiling water over noodles in bowl and stir to separate. Let noodles soak until soft and pliable but not fully tender, stirring once half-way through soaking, 12 to 15 minutes. Drain noodles, then rinse with cold water until water runs clear. Shake to remove excess water and set aside.

2. Meanwhile, whisk chili crisp, vinegar, and 2 tablespoons vegetable oil together in bowl; set aside. Pat steaks dry with paper towels and sprinkle with ½ teaspoon salt and ¼ teaspoon pepper. Rub steaks all over with half of reserved chili crisp sauce.

3. Heat 1 tablespoon oil in 12-inch nonstick skillet over medium-high heat until just smoking. Add steaks and cook until well browned and meat registers 120 to 125 degrees (for medium-rare), 2 to 3 minutes per side. Transfer steaks to cutting board, tent loosely with aluminum foil, and let rest while cooking green beans.

4. Heat fat remaining in skillet over medium-high heat until shimmering. Stir in green beans, ¼ teaspoon salt, and ⅛ teaspoon pepper and cook until spotty brown, 3 to 5 minutes. Add 2 tablespoons water, cover, and cook until beans are bright green and crisp-tender, about 2 minutes. Uncover and cook until water evaporates, 1 to 2 minutes.

5. Off heat, add noodles and remaining reserved chili crisp sauce to beans in skillet and toss to combine. Season with salt and pepper to taste. Slice steaks thin against grain and serve with noodles.

For a slightly different, but no less comforting, spin on pasta with meatballs, I like to mix it up by swapping in pearl couscous for spaghetti; ground lamb for beef; and cherry tomatoes for canned tomatoes. I mix together lamb, garlic, and a moisture-ensuring panade (made with seasoned bread crumbs for an added boost of flavor), form the meatballs, and pop them into the oven. While they cook, I sauté lots of sliced garlic in oil, which not only creates a garlicky base for toasting the couscous but also yields garlic chips for a crispy garnish. Cherry tomatoes, added to the couscous while it cooks, burst open to create a just-saucy-enough sauce.

—CAMILA CHAPARRO, *Test Cook*

Lamb Meatballs with Pearl Couscous

SERVES 4   TOTAL TIME: 40 MINUTES

6 tablespoons seasoned panko bread crumbs

1 pound ground lamb or 80 percent lean ground beef

9 garlic cloves (8 sliced thin, 1 minced)

2 cups pearl couscous

1 pound cherry or grape tomatoes

STAPLE INGREDIENTS:

Extra-virgin olive oil
Table salt
Pepper

1. Adjust oven rack to upper-middle position and heat oven to 450 degrees. Set wire rack in aluminum foil–lined rimmed baking sheet. Mash panko and 3 tablespoons water into paste in large bowl. Add lamb, minced garlic, ½ teaspoon salt, and ¼ teaspoon pepper and gently knead with hands until combined. Pinch off and roll mixture into 16 tightly packed 1½-inch-wide meatballs and arrange evenly on prepared rack. Roast until meatballs are lightly browned and cooked through, 17 to 20 minutes.

2. Meanwhile, heat 3 tablespoons olive oil and sliced garlic in large saucepan over medium heat, stirring constantly once garlic starts to sizzle. Cook until garlic is light golden brown, 3 to 5 minutes. Using slotted spoon, transfer garlic to paper towel–lined plate and season with salt to taste; set aside for serving.

3. Add couscous to remaining oil in saucepan and cook over medium heat, stirring frequently, until half of grains are golden brown, 5 to 6 minutes. Stir in tomatoes, 2¼ cups water, ½ teaspoon salt, and ⅛ teaspoon pepper and bring to simmer. Simmer until couscous is tender, about 15 minutes, stirring once halfway through. Adjust consistency with hot water as needed and season with salt and pepper to taste. Drizzle couscous with olive oil to taste and sprinkle with reserved garlic chips. Serve immediately with meatballs.

In Valencian and Catalan cuisine, fideuá is a classic seafood dish similar to paella, but made with short, thin dried pasta (fideos) instead of rice. For my rendition, I first brown fideos to develop deep toasty flavor, then simmer the pasta in a stock that I make from the (usually discarded) shrimp shells. I toss it all together with licorice-y fennel and fat, juicy shrimp (I like to use extra-large shrimp, 21 to 25 per pound) and slide it under the broiler until the shrimp are cooked through and the noodles on top get nice and crispy. If you can't find fideos, you can substitute thin spaghetti broken into 1- to 2-inch pieces (wrap bundle of pasta in a clean dish towel before breaking to keep things tidy).

—LEAH COLINS, *Test Cook*

Fideos with Shrimp and Fennel

SERVES 4   TOTAL TIME: 50 MINUTES

1½   pounds shrimp, peeled and deveined, shells reserved

8   ounces fideos (2 cups)

1   fennel bulb, 2 tablespoons fronds minced, stalks discarded, bulb halved, cored, and sliced thin

4   garlic cloves, minced

1½   teaspoons smoked paprika

STAPLE INGREDIENTS:

Extra-virgin olive oil
Table salt
Pepper

1. Adjust oven rack 5 to 6 inches from broiler element and heat broiler. Heat 1 tablespoon olive oil in large saucepan over high heat until shimmering. Add shrimp shells and cook, stirring frequently, until spotty brown, 2 to 4 minutes. Carefully add 3¾ cups water and ½ teaspoon salt, scraping up any browned bits, and bring to boil. Reduce heat to low and simmer for 5 minutes. Strain stock through fine-mesh strainer set over large bowl, pressing on solids to extract as much liquid as possible; discard solids and reserve stock.

2. Meanwhile, toss pasta and 2 teaspoons oil in broiler-safe 12-inch skillet until evenly coated. Toast over medium heat, stirring often, until browned and pasta has nutty aroma, 6 to 10 minutes; transfer to bowl.

3. Add 2 tablespoons oil to now-empty skillet and heat over medium-high heat until shimmering. Add sliced fennel and ¼ teaspoon salt and cook until softened and beginning to brown, 4 to 6 minutes. Stir in garlic and smoked paprika and cook until fragrant, about 1 minute. Stir in shrimp broth, pasta, ½ teaspoon pepper, and ¼ teaspoon salt. Bring to simmer, then reduce heat to maintain simmer and cook, stirring occasionally, until most of liquid had been absorbed and pasta is just tender, 8 to 10 minutes.

4. Stir shrimp into pasta then transfer skillet to oven and broil until shrimp are opaque throughout and surface of pasta is dry with crisped, browned spots, 5 to 7 minutes. Remove from oven and let sit for 5 minutes. Sprinkle with minced fennel fronds and serve immediately.

There's a Colombian dish (arroz con titoté) that starts by reducing coconut milk until the coconut solids are toasted and nutty. I use that same method for this dish, then add a bit of liquid to build a rich sauce to coat rice noodles. To pair with the faintly sweet noodles, I toss in chunks of tender shrimp (extra-large shrimp, 21 to 25 per pound, is best) and crispy snow peas. Banana peppers and their brine are the perfect thing to cut through the richness with a spicy, vinegary kick. Make sure to use full-fat coconut milk with no additives or preservatives or it won't reduce and caramelize correctly.

—CAMILA CHAPARRO, *Test Cook*

Coconut Rice Noodles with Shrimp and Snow Peas

SERVES 4   TOTAL TIME: 30 MINUTES

8 ounces (¼-inch-wide) rice noodles

1 (14-ounce) can coconut milk

1 pound shrimp, peeled, deveined, and chopped

8 ounces snow peas, strings removed and halved crosswise

⅓ cup jarred banana pepper rings, chopped, plus 3 tablespoons brine and extra brine for serving

STAPLE INGREDIENTS:

Table salt
Pepper

1. Pour 2 quarts boiling water over noodles in bowl and stir to separate. Let noodles soak until soft and pliable but not fully tender, stirring once halfway through soaking, 8 to 10 minutes. Reserve ½ cup soaking water, then drain noodles and rinse with cold water until water runs clear. Shake to remove excess water and set noodles aside.

2. Meanwhile, cook coconut milk in Dutch oven over medium-high heat, partially covered and stirring occasionally, until reduced by about three-quarters and beginning to sputter, 9 to 12 minutes. Reduce heat to medium. Uncover pot and cook, stirring frequently, until fat separates from coconut solids, 2 to 3 minutes. Continue to cook, stirring frequently, until coconut solids turn deep brown (solids will stick to Dutch oven), 3 to 4 minutes longer.

3. Pat shrimp dry with paper towels. Add shrimp and snow peas to Dutch oven and cook until shrimp are pink around edges, 1 to 2 minutes. Stir in rice noodles, banana peppers and brine, and ¼ cup reserved soaking water. Cook until noodles are warmed through and tender and shrimp is opaque, about 2 minutes. Adjust consistency with remaining reserved soaking water as needed and season with salt, pepper, and extra banana pepper brine to taste. Serve.

This lightly sauced noodle stir-fry is inspired by Singapore noodles, a dish that is actually native to Hong Kong (not Singapore), where curry powder is a common ingredient. Shiitake mushrooms and shrimp add bulk and meatiness, while the mushroom stems and shrimp shells simmer to make an umami-rich stock to serve as the base of a sauce (along with soy sauce and a heavy dose of curry powder). I stir-fry everything separately to ensure each ingredient cooks properly, and then toss it all together with the sauce before serving.

—LEAH COLINS, *Test Cook*

Curried Noodles with Shrimp and Mushrooms

SERVES 4   TOTAL TIME: 40 MINUTES

1   pound shrimp, peeled and deveined, shells reserved and shrimp chopped

10   ounces shiitake mushrooms, stems reserved and caps cut into 1-inch pieces

8   ounces rice vermicelli

2   tablespoons curry powder

3   tablespoons soy sauce

STAPLE INGREDIENTS:

Vegetable oil
Table salt
Pepper

1. Heat 1 tablespoon vegetable oil in large saucepan over high heat until shimmering. Add shrimp shells and cook, stirring frequently, until spotty brown, 2 to 4 minutes. Carefully add 1½ cups water, shiitake stems, and ¼ teaspoon salt and bring to boil. Reduce heat to low and simmer for 7 minutes. Strain stock through fine-mesh strainer set over bowl, pressing on solids to extract as much liquid as possible; discard solids and reserve stock. Meanwhile, pour 2 quarts boiling water over noodles in bowl and let sit, stirring occasionally, until tender, about 5 minutes. Drain noodles, rinse with cold water, and drain again; set aside.

2. Heat 1 tablespoon oil in 12-inch nonstick skillet over medium-high heat until shimmering. Add shrimp and cook until browned and just cooked through, 2 to 3 minutes, stirring halfway through; transfer to serving bowl. Heat 1 tablespoon oil in now-empty skillet over medium-high heat until shimmering. Add mushroom caps and 2 tablespoons water, cover, and cook until just softened, about 3 minutes. Uncover and cook until beginning to brown, about 3 minutes; add to bowl with shrimp.

3. Heat 2 tablespoons oil in again-empty skillet over medium-high heat until shimmering. Add curry powder and cook until fragrant, about 1 minute. Off heat, add shrimp stock and soy sauce. Bring to simmer over medium-high heat, stir in noodles, and cook until liquid is absorbed, about 2 minutes. Add noodles to bowl with shrimp and mushrooms and toss to combine. Season with salt and pepper to taste. Serve.

Aromatic sage and rich hazelnuts infuse a browned butter sauce that envelops crispy cauliflower and tender pasta. The bell-shaped noodles, campanelle, are not only beautiful, but do a great job of capturing a special sauce made with just starchy water and butter that emulsifies and clings to every forkful. Lemon zest and juice add brightness and acidity. For a garnish that is as delicious as it is beautiful, I fry whole sage leaves and arrange them on top just before serving (a favorite from my restaurant days!).

—CARMEN DONGO, *Test Cook*

Cauliflower Pasta with Browned Butter–Sage Sauce

SERVES 4 TO 6   TOTAL TIME: 35 MINUTES

- 1 **pound campanelle or orecchiette**
- 1 **head cauliflower (2 pounds), cored and cut into 1-inch florets**
- ½ **cup hazelnuts, skinned, peeled, and chopped coarse**
- 2 **tablespoons chopped fresh sage, plus 12 fresh leaves**
- ½ **teaspoon grated lemon zest plus 1 tablespoon juice, plus lemon wedges for serving**

STAPLE INGREDIENTS:

**Extra-virgin olive oil
Unsalted butter
Table salt**

1. Bring 2 quarts water to boil in large pot. Add pasta and 1½ teaspoons salt and cook, stirring often, until al dente. Reserve 1½ cups cooking water, then drain pasta and return to now-empty pot.

2. Meanwhile, heat 2 tablespoons olive oil in 12-inch skillet over medium-high heat until shimmering. Add cauliflower and 1 teaspoon salt and cook, stirring occasionally, until florets are crisp-tender and browned in spots, 10 to 12 minutes. Transfer to bowl and set aside.

3. Melt 6 tablespoons butter in now-empty skillet over medium heat, then add hazelnuts and ¼ teaspoon salt. Cook, swirling skillet constantly, until butter begins to brown and has nutty aroma, 1 to 2 minutes. Add chopped and whole sage leaves and cook until sage darkens in color and is fragrant, about 1 minute. Remove from heat and transfer whole sage leaves to paper towel–lined plate, leaving remaining sage and browned butter in skillet.

4. Add 1 cup reserved cooking water to skillet with browned butter mixture and bring to boil over high heat, scraping up any browned bits. Remove from heat and stir in lemon zest and juice. Add browned butter sauce and reserved cauliflower to pasta in pot and toss to coat. Adjust consistency with remaining reserved cooking water as needed and season with salt and pepper to taste. Serve with lemon wedges and reserved whole sage leaves.

Pesto is one of the best sauces to riff on—depending on the season and what I have on hand, I sneak all kinds of vegetables into it. But this broccoli rendition may be my favorite. I first blanch some broccoli (stalks and all) and puree a portion with tons of basil and nuts to create an aromatic, vibrant green sauce, while saving the remaining broccoli to add some heft to the final salad. I boil pasta in the leftover water from cooking the broccoli (hello timesaver!), let it cool a bit, and toss everything together. A sprinkling of extra chopped nuts and some raisins give great crunch and sweet appeal.

—LEAH COLINS, *Test Cook*

Broccoli-Basil Pasta Salad

SERVES 4 TO 6   TOTAL TIME: 50 MINUTES

1 pound broccoli, florets cut into 1-inch pieces, stalks peeled and sliced ¼ inch thick

1 pound gemelli or rotini

3 cups fresh basil leaves

¾ cup pine nuts or chopped cashews, toasted, divided

½ cup raisins or chopped dried apricots

STAPLE INGREDIENTS:

Extra-virgin olive oil
Table salt
Pepper

1. Fill large bowl halfway with ice and water; set aside. Bring 4 quarts water to boil in large pot. Add 1 tablespoon salt and broccoli stalks and cook for 1 minute. Add florets and cook until stalks and florets are tender, about 2 minutes longer. Using slotted spoon, remove broccoli and transfer to ice bath (do not discard boiling water). Let broccoli sit until chilled, about 5 minutes, then drain and pat dry with paper towels; set aside.

2. Add pasta to reserved boiling water and cook, stirring often, until al dente. Reserve ½ cup cooking water then drain pasta. Toss pasta with 1 tablespoon olive oil and spread in single layer on rimmed baking sheet. Let cool for 15 minutes.

3. Meanwhile, process 1 cup cooled broccoli, basil, ½ cup pine nuts, and ¾ teaspoon salt in food processor until smooth, about 30 seconds, scraping down sides of bowl as needed. Add 6 tablespoons oil and process until thoroughly combined.

4. Toss pasta with broccoli-basil sauce and ¼ cup reserved cooking water until sauce evenly coats pasta. Stir in remaining cooled broccoli and raisins and season with salt and pepper to taste. Sprinkle with remaining ¼ cup pine nuts. Serve.

Making gnocchi from scratch was always a Sunday tradition in my family. The idea of using store-bought gnocchi would have been frowned upon, to say the least! But the quality of gnocchi has come a long way since then, so I decided to make a new tradition. For restaurant appeal in an easy, semi-home-cooked package, I make a blush sauce for packaged gnocchi out of sun-dried tomatoes and ricotta cheese (just 2 ingredients!). Seasoned panko bread crumbs simply toasted in the microwave bring a final contrasting crispy bite to the creamy gnocchi.

—LEAH COLINS, *Test Cook*

Gnocchi with Sun-Dried Tomatoes, Ricotta, and Spinach

SERVES 4 TO 6   **TOTAL TIME: 30 MINUTES**

2   pounds vacuum-packed, refrigerated, or frozen gnocchi

½   cup seasoned panko bread crumbs

½   cup oil-packed sun-dried tomatoes, patted dry and chopped, plus ¼ cup tomato oil

8   ounces (8 cups) baby spinach

8   ounces (1 cup) whole-milk ricotta cheese, room temperature

STAPLE INGREDIENTS:

Extra-virgin olive oil
Table salt
Pepper

1. Bring 4 quarts water to boil in large pot. Add gnocchi and 1 tablespoon salt and cook, stirring often, until just cooked through. Reserve 1½ cups cooking water, then drain gnocchi and set aside. Wipe pot dry with paper towels.

2. Meanwhile, toss panko with 1 tablespoon olive oil in bowl. Microwave panko, stirring occasionally, until deep golden brown, 1 to 4 minutes; set aside to cool.

3. Heat tomato oil in now-empty pot over medium heat until shimmering. Add sun-dried tomatoes and spinach, 1 handful at a time and cook, stirring constantly, until spinach is uniformly wilted, about 1 minute. Stir in cooked gnocchi and ½ cup reserved cooking water and toss to coat.

4. Off heat, stir in ricotta until well combined. Adjust consistency with remaining 1 cup reserved cooking water as needed and season with salt and pepper to taste. Sprinkle individual portions with toasted bread crumbs. Serve.

Creating complex flavors doesn't have to be complicated. For this weeknight-friendly soba noodle salad, grassy asparagus cooks in the same pot as earthy soba noodles (saving on dishes), while savory miso and citrusy-spicy Japanese shichimi togarashi create a simple but superflavorful dressing. Strips of crispy nori round out the salad with sweet brininess. If I'm feeling generous I'll share this with my family, but more often than not I keep it all for myself—it's perfect for keeping in the fridge for quick cold lunches throughout the week.

—CAMILA CHAPARRO, *Test Cook*

Shichimi Togarashi Soba Noodles with Asparagus

SERVES 4   TOTAL TIME: 35 MINUTES

¼ cup white miso

1 teaspoon shichimi togarashi, divided

2 sheets toasted nori

1 pound asparagus, trimmed and sliced 1 inch thick on bias

12 ounces soba noodles or spaghetti

STAPLE INGREDIENTS:

Extra-virgin olive oil
Table salt

1. Whisk miso, ½ teaspoon shichimi togarashi, 3 tablespoons olive oil, and 6 tablespoons hot water together in large bowl until smooth; set aside. Using scissors, cut nori sheets into four 2-inch strips. Stack strips and cut crosswise into thin strips; set aside.

2. Fill large bowl halfway with ice and water; set aside. Bring 4 quarts water to boil in large pot. Add 1 tablespoon salt and asparagus and cook until bright green and crisp-tender, 1 to 2 minutes. Using slotted spoon transfer to ice bath (do not discard boiling water). Let asparagus sit until chilled, about 5 minutes, then drain and pat dry with paper towels. Add to bowl with miso mixture.

3. Add noodles to reserved boiling water and cook, stirring often, until al dente. Drain noodles and rinse thoroughly with cold water. Transfer noodles and half of nori strips to bowl with miso mixture and toss to coat. Sprinkle with remaining ½ teaspoon shichimi togarashi and remaining nori and serve.

Meatless Mondays

Canned beans are something I always have on hand. And that's lucky for me (and my taste buds), because a can of beans is so much more than just beans. In this hearty soup, the bean liquid does the heavy lifting, providing body and silky texture, which means you really don't need a lot in the way of herbs or aromatics to make the soup sing. A base of smoky, fruity chipotle chile in adobo sauce brings heat and spice, and plain Greek yogurt and lime add brightness and a little tang.

—BRENNA DONOVAN, *Editor*

Black Bean Soup

SERVES 4 TO 6   TOTAL TIME: 25 MINUTES

4   (15-ounce) cans black beans, undrained

4   cups vegetable or chicken broth

2–3   tablespoons minced canned chipotle chile in adobo sauce

½   cup plain Greek yogurt or sour cream

1   teaspoon grated lime zest, plus lime wedges for serving

STAPLE INGREDIENTS:

Table salt
Pepper

1. Bring beans and their liquid, broth, and chipotle to boil in Dutch oven. Reduce heat to medium-low, cover, and simmer, stirring occasionally, until beans begin to break down, 20 to 25 minutes. Using potato masher, coarsely mash beans in pot. Adjust consistency with extra hot water as needed.

2. Stir in yogurt and lime zest and season with salt and pepper to taste. Serve with lime wedges.

The not-so-secret ingredient in this dressed-up-can-of-beans soup is garlic—a whopping 17 cloves do the bulk of the work to flavor the soup (see page 129 for a trick for peeling lots of garlic). But it's not just in-your-face sharpness: Because the garlic is treated in different ways (broiled with broccoli rabe, dry-toasted still in its skin, and turned into garlic chips to toss with lemon zest and chives for garnish), it practically transforms into three entirely different ingredients. A spin in the blender makes this chickpea soup smooth and velvety, and an acidic splash of lemon juice perks things up.

—CARMEN DONGO, *Test Cook*

Creamy Chickpea, Broccoli Rabe, and Garlic Soup

SERVES 4 TO 6   TOTAL TIME: 35 MINUTES

1   pound broccoli rabe, trimmed and cut into 1-inch lengths

17 garlic cloves (1 minced, 8 sliced, 8 unpeeled)

1   teaspoon grated lemon zest plus 2 tablespoons juice

3   tablespoons minced fresh chives, divided

2   (15-ounce) cans chickpeas, undrained

STAPLE INGREDIENTS:

Extra-virgin olive oil
Table salt

1. Adjust oven rack 4 inches from broiler element and heat broiler. Brush rimmed baking sheet with 1 tablespoon olive oil. Toss broccoli rabe with 2 tablespoons oil, minced garlic, and ½ teaspoon salt, then spread in even layer over prepared sheet. Broil until exposed leaves are well browned, about 2 minutes. Toss to expose unbrowned leaves then return sheet to oven and broil until most leaves are well browned and stalks are crisp-tender, about 2 minutes; set aside.

2. Heat 3 tablespoons oil and sliced garlic in large saucepan over medium heat, stirring constantly once garlic starts to sizzle. Cook until garlic is light golden, 3 to 5 minutes. Using slotted spoon, transfer garlic to bowl and toss with lemon zest and 1 teaspoon chives. Set aside.

3. Carefully wipe out saucepan. Toast unpeeled garlic in now-empty saucepan over medium heat until skins are beginning to brown, about 5 minutes. Remove from saucepan and let cool. Peel garlic then return to now-empty saucepan along with chickpeas and their liquid, 2½ cups water, and ½ teaspoon salt. Bring to simmer and cook over medium-low heat until chickpeas begin to break down, 5 to 7 minutes.

4. Working in batches, process soup in blender until smooth, about 2 minutes. Return soup to again-empty saucepan, stir in broccoli rabe, and adjust consistency with extra hot water as needed. Cook over medium heat until warmed through, about 2 minutes. Stir in remaining chives and lemon juice. Serve with garlic chips.

YOU CAN SERVE WITH
**CRUSTY BREAD OR
A SIMPLE SALAD**

Here, the sweet flavors of carrots, ginger, and coconut milk meet savory crispy tofu and unsalted peanuts. I'm always looking for easy ways to work more vegetarian meals into my weeknight dinners, and I love how easy this soup is to put together. Grating the ginger allows for an even infusion of flavor, and the coconut milk adds an element of decadence. The secret to both the soup's silky texture as well as its heartiness is tofu—I crisp some in the saucepan, then blend more into the soup. Although time-intensive, draining and pressing the tofu will guarantee crispy tofu, so don't skimp on this step.

—CARMEN DONGO, *Test Cook*

Gingery Coconut Carrot Soup with Tofu Croutons

SERVES 4 TOTAL TIME: 1 HOUR 5 MINUTES

14 ounces extra-firm tofu, cut lengthwise into 3 equal slabs, divided

1 pound carrots, peeled and cut into ½-inch pieces

1 tablespoon grated fresh ginger

1 (14-ounce) can coconut milk

½ cup unsalted dry-roasted peanuts, chopped

STAPLE INGREDIENTS:

Extra-virgin olive oil
Table salt
Pepper

1. Place tofu on paper towel–lined plate and let drain for 20 minutes, then gently press dry with paper towels. Sprinkle with ¼ teaspoon salt and ⅛ teaspoon pepper. Heat 2 tablespoons olive oil in large saucepan over medium-high heat until shimmering. Add 2 tofu slabs and cook, flipping as needed, until lightly browned on both sides, 6 to 8 minutes. Transfer tofu to cutting board and cut into ½-inch pieces; set aside.

2. Add carrots and ½ teaspoon salt to oil left in saucepan and cook, stirring occasionally, until lightly browned, 6 to 8 minutes. Stir in ginger and cook until fragrant, about 1 minute. Stir in 1½ cups water and coconut milk, scraping up any browned bits and bring to simmer. Cook, covered, over medium-low heat until carrots are tender, 10 to 15 minutes.

3. Transfer 1 cup soup and remaining tofu slab to blender and process until smooth, about 2 minutes. Stir pureed soup and reserved browned tofu into remaining soup in saucepan and adjust consistency with extra hot water as needed. Season with salt and pepper to taste. Serve with chopped peanuts.

YOU CAN SERVE WITH
RICE OR NAAN BREAD

Dried red lentils are always something I keep in my pantry—they're packed with protein and are perfect for a quick, nutritious meal. I especially love using them to make dal, a comforting Indian dish made from dried lentils or other legumes. For my take on palak dal (palak means "spinach" in Hindi), I start by cooking the lentils with fresh ginger, whisk them vigorously to create a rustic, porridge-like stew, and then stir in a few handfuls of fresh spinach. For a crunchy garnish, I fry shallots in the microwave, and then bloom garam masala in the still-hot leftover shallot oil to create a spiced-up finishing drizzle.

—RUSSELL SELANDER, *Test Cook*

Spiced Red Lentils with Spinach and Crispy Shallots

SERVES 4   TOTAL TIME: 45 MINUTES

10½ ounces (1½ cups) dried red lentils, picked over and rinsed

1 tablespoon grated fresh ginger

3 shallots, sliced thin

1 tablespoon garam masala

6 ounces (6 cups) baby spinach

STAPLE INGREDIENTS:

Vegetable oil
Table salt

1. Bring 4½ cups water, lentils, and ginger to boil in large saucepan. Simmer vigorously, stirring occasionally, until lentils are soft and beginning to break down, 18 to 20 minutes, adjusting heat as needed.

2. While lentils simmer, microwave shallots and ½ cup vegetable oil in medium bowl for 5 minutes. Stir and continue to microwave in 2-minute increments until beginning to brown (2 to 6 minutes). Repeat stirring and microwaving in 30-second increments until golden brown (30 seconds to 2 minutes). Using slotted spoon, transfer shallots to paper towel–lined plate and season with salt to taste; stir garam masala into 3 tablespoons hot shallot oil and set aside. Discard remaining shallot oil or reserve for another use.

3. Whisk lentils vigorously until coarsely pureed, about 30 seconds. Continue to cook until lentils have consistency of loose polenta or oatmeal, about 5 minutes longer. Stir in spinach and 1½ teaspoons salt and continue to cook until spinach is wilted, about 30 seconds. Season with salt and pepper to taste. Serve with garam masala oil and crispy shallots.

Broccoli florets and canned chickpeas get nice and crispy in a skillet, delivering roasted flavor without having to turn on my oven. For a creamy dressing without any mayo, I mash together avocado, olive oil, and pickled jalapeño brine to coat every inch of the warm broccoli and chickpeas. (I also set some avocado aside to toss with the salad at the end.) To balance it all, thinly sliced shallot and pickled jalapeños add a sharp bite that cuts through the rich creaminess of the dressing.

—LEAH COLINS, *Test Cook*

Warm Broccoli, Chickpea, and Avocado Salad

SERVES 4   TOTAL TIME: 45 MINUTES

2   avocados, halved, pitted, and cut into ½-inch pieces, divided

½   cup pickled jalapeños, chopped, plus ¼ cup brine

1½ pounds broccoli florets, cut into 2-inch pieces

2   (15-ounce) cans chickpeas, rinsed

1   large shallot, sliced thin

STAPLE INGREDIENTS:

Extra-virgin olive oil
Table salt
Pepper

1. Mash ½ cup avocado, jalapeño brine, and 2 tablespoons olive oil in serving bowl with fork until combined; set dressing aside. Heat 3 tablespoons oil in 12-inch nonstick skillet over medium heat until shimmering. Add broccoli, ¾ teaspoon salt, and ½ teaspoon pepper. Cook, stirring occasionally, until broccoli is dark brown and crispy in spots, about 20 minutes. Add to bowl with reserved dressing.

2. Add 2 tablespoons oil to now-empty skillet and heat over medium-high heat until shimmering. Add chickpeas, ¼ teaspoon salt, and ¼ teaspoon pepper and cook until lightly browned, 6 to 10 minutes. Add to bowl with broccoli and dressing.

3. Add shallot, pickled jalapeños, and remaining avocado to bowl and stir to combine. Season with salt and pepper to taste. Serve.

Nutty, chewy farro is one of the fastest-cooking whole grains around, making it perfect for a good-for-you grain salad on the fly. While the farro cooks, broil cubed eggplant until it's nice and brown, which brings essential meatiness and savory, caramelized flavor to the salad. A hefty amount of jarred roasted red peppers adds sweetness and extra veggie goodness. Once the farro is cooled, toss everything together with thinly sliced scallions and a lemony dressing that permeates the whole dish.

—RUSSELL SELANDER, *Test Cook*

Farro Salad with Roasted Eggplant

SERVES 4 TO 6   TOTAL TIME: 50 MINUTES

1½   cups whole farro

1½   pounds eggplant, cut into ½-inch pieces

1   teaspoon grated lemon zest plus 1 tablespoon juice

1½   cups jarred roasted red peppers, rinsed, patted dry, and cut into ½-inch pieces

3   scallions, sliced thin

STAPLE INGREDIENTS:

Extra-virgin olive oil
Table salt
Pepper

1. Adjust oven rack 4 inches from broiler element and heat broiler. Bring 4 quarts water to boil in large pot. Add farro and 1 tablespoon salt and cook until grains are tender with slight chew, 15 to 30 minutes. Drain farro, spread onto rimmed baking sheet, and let cool for 15 minutes.

2. Meanwhile, toss eggplant with 3 tablespoons olive oil, then transfer to aluminum foil–lined rimmed baking sheet and spread into even layer. Broil eggplant until well browned, 15 to 17 minutes, stirring halfway through.

3. Whisk 3 tablespoons oil and lemon zest and juice together in large bowl. Add cooled farro, eggplant, red peppers, scallions, ½ teaspoon salt, and ¼ teaspoon pepper and toss to combine. Season with salt and pepper to taste. Serve.

Whenever I make rice, I always cook more than I'll need. A giant pot of rice is the gift that keeps on giving, and in this case, that gift is a garlicky, savory, veggie-packed meal. (See pages 249–251 if you don't have any leftover rice at the ready.) Garlic does the heavy lifting flavor-wise here, with help from briny, pungent fish sauce that perfumes the whole situation. (See page 129 for a tip on how to easily peel a lot of garlic.) The best part, though? Those crunchy hits of rice peppered throughout, where the lime juice and fish sauce concentrate into tiny umami bombs. Cooking the rice undisturbed right at the end is key to getting those magical crispy bits, so don't get stir-crazy.

—BRENNA DONOVAN, *Editor*

Garlicky Fried Rice with Bok Choy

SERVES 4 TO 6   TOTAL TIME: 45 MINUTES

1½ pounds baby bok choy, halved lengthwise and sliced crosswise ½ inch thick

10 garlic cloves, minced

4 cups cooked rice

2 tablespoons fish sauce

1 teaspoon grated lime zest plus 1½ tablespoons juice

STAPLE INGREDIENTS:

Vegetable oil
Table salt
Pepper

1. Heat 1 tablespoon vegetable oil in 12-inch nonstick skillet over medium-high heat until just smoking. Add bok choy and ½ teaspoon salt and cook until beginning to soften and char in spots, 2 to 4 minutes. Stir in garlic and cook until fragrant, about 30 seconds. Stir in rice, 2 tablespoons oil, fish sauce, lime zest and juice, and ¼ teaspoon pepper.

2. Firmly press rice mixture into compact, even layer. Cover and cook, without stirring, until rice begins to crisp, about 2 minutes. Uncover, reduce heat to medium, and continue to cook until bottom of rice is golden brown, 4 to 6 minutes. Season with salt and pepper to taste and serve.

For a quick and filling lunch while developing recipes from home, I've been turning to this fast and easy quinoa salad that I can throw together with ingredients I almost always have on hand. And best of all, there's hardly any cooking involved beyond making the quinoa. Toasting the quinoa with a little garlic before adding water is a great way to infuse flavor right from the beginning. Once the quinoa is cooked, stir in some arugula for a zero-prep way to bulk things up. Add a quick garlicky yogurt sauce and some crunchy almonds, and you're in lunch-break heaven.

—LEAH COLINS, *Test Cook*

Quinoa with Arugula, Almonds, and Yogurt Sauce

SERVES 4   TOTAL TIME: 40 MINUTES

½   cup plain yogurt

4   garlic cloves (1 minced, 3 sliced thin)

1½   cups prewashed white quinoa

4   ounces (4 cups) baby arugula

½   cup sliced almonds, toasted; or chopped smoked almonds

STAPLE INGREDIENTS:

Extra-virgin olive oil
Table salt
Pepper

1. Whisk yogurt, 2 tablespoons olive oil, 1 tablespoon water, and minced garlic together in bowl. Season with salt and pepper to taste; set sauce aside until ready to serve.

2. Heat 2 tablespoons oil in large saucepan over medium-high heat until shimmering. Add sliced garlic and cook until light golden and fragrant, about 1 minute. Add quinoa and cook until very fragrant and making continuous popping sounds, 3 to 5 minutes. Stir in 1¾ cups water and ½ teaspoon salt and bring to simmer. Reduce heat to low, cover, and simmer until quinoa is tender and water is absorbed, 18 to 22 minutes, stirring once halfway through cooking.

3. Remove pot from heat and let sit, covered, for 5 minutes. Gently fluff with fork then stir in arugula and season with salt and pepper to taste. Sprinkle with almonds and drizzle with reserved yogurt sauce. Serve.

Stuffed acorn squash is a great way to get a complete meal in one tidy package, and this version doesn't skimp on flavor with the addition of supersavory ras el hanout and bright pomegranate molasses. Add to that some browned butter and pine nuts and you've got a deeply flavorful Mediterranean-inspired dinner. Precooking the squash is essential here, but on a busy weeknight I often don't have the patience for roasting. So I turn to my microwave since it does a great job of cooking the squash in record time. Do not use coarse or medium-grind bulgur in this recipe.

—STEPHANIE PIXLEY, *Editor*

Bulgur-Stuffed Acorn Squash with Ras el Hanout

SERVES 4   TOTAL TIME: 50 MINUTES

- 2 acorn squashes (1½ pounds each), halved pole to pole and seeded
- ½ cup fine-grind bulgur
- ½ cup pine nuts or chopped walnuts
- 2 teaspoons ras el hanout
- 2 tablespoons pomegranate molasses

STAPLE INGREDIENTS:

Unsalted butter
Table salt

---

1. Adjust oven rack to upper-middle position and heat broiler. Line rimmed baking sheet with aluminum foil. Sprinkle cut sides of squash halves with ¾ teaspoon salt and place cut side down on large plate. Microwave until tender and offering no resistance when pierced with paring knife, 15 to 20 minutes. Transfer squash halves cut side up to prepared sheet and let cool for 5 to 10 minutes.

2. Using spoon, scoop flesh from each squash half into bowl, leaving about ⅛-inch thickness of flesh; set flesh and squash shells aside. Pour ¾ boiling water over bulgur and ½ teaspoon salt in large bowl. Cover and let sit until tender, about 5 minutes. Fluff with fork and set aside.

3. Melt 4 tablespoons butter in 12-inch skillet over medium heat. Cook, swirling skillet constantly, until butter begins to brown and has nutty aroma, 1 to 2 minutes. Add pine nuts and ras el hanout and cook, stirring constantly, until fragrant and foamy, 1 to 2 minutes. Stir in reserved squash and cook until well combined and beginning to brown, 3 to 4 minutes. Fold into cooked bulgur in bowl, then mound mixture evenly in squash shells.

4. Broil stuffed squash until beginning to brown, about 5 minutes. Drizzle with pomegranate molasses and serve.

With three young kids, sometimes the simplest dinners are the best, but that doesn't mean I want something snooze-worthy. This take on haluski, the ultracomforting Eastern-European cabbage and egg noodle dish, is always a slam dunk (who can say no to buttery noodles?). I sauté cabbage and onion in butter to develop some nice browning—with caraway seeds for mild anise notes—then add cooked noodles right into the skillet with some reserved pasta water so they can soak up all of the good stuff. Finally, I top each portion with a fried egg, the runny yolk adding creaminess and saucy cohesion.

—RUSSELL SELANDER, *Test Cook*

Sautéed Buttery Egg Noodles with Cabbage and Fried Eggs

SERVES 4   TOTAL TIME: 40 MINUTES

8   ounces egg noodles

3   cups coarsely chopped green cabbage

1   small onion, sliced thin

¾   teaspoon caraway seeds

4   large eggs

STAPLE INGREDIENTS:

Unsalted butter
Vegetable oil
Table salt
Pepper

1. Bring 4 quarts water to boil in Dutch oven. Add noodles and 1 tablespoon salt and cook, stirring often, until al dente, 10 to 12 minutes. Reserve 1 cup cooking water, then drain noodles and set aside. Wipe out pot.

2. Melt 3 tablespoons butter in now-empty pot over medium-high heat. Add cabbage, onion, and ¼ teaspoon salt and cook, stirring occasionally, until vegetables are softened and beginning to brown, 6 to 8 minutes. Stir in caraway seeds and cook until fragrant, about 30 seconds. Stir in ½ teaspoon pepper, reserved cooked noodles, and ½ cup reserved cooking water, scraping up any browned bits, and simmer until reduced slightly, 1 to 2 minutes. Adjust consistency with remaining reserved cooking water as needed and season with salt and pepper to taste.

3. Meanwhile, heat 1 tablespoon vegetable oil in 12-inch nonstick skillet over medium-high heat until shimmering. Add eggs to skillet and sprinkle with ⅛ teaspoon salt and ⅛ teaspoon pepper. Cover and cook for 1 minute. Remove skillet from heat and let sit, covered, for 15 to 45 seconds for runny yolks, 45 to 60 seconds for soft but set yolks, or about 2 minutes for medium-set yolks. Serve noodles topped with egg.

My favorite part about this simple, vegetable-forward dinner is that it's hardly more work than assembling pre-prepped or jarred ingredients (especially if you buy your zucchini already spiralized—if not, you'll need 2 pounds of zucchini). A quick sauté tames the raw qualities of the zucchini and jarred artichokes without turning them to mush. Marinated feta brings some tangy creaminess, and its herby oil mingles with the moistness of the zucchini and bright lemon juice to ensure the noodles are thoroughly coated. Finally, a sprinkling of pine nuts elevates everything to a meal that will keep you full.

—RUSSELL SELANDER, *Test Cook*

Lemony Zoodles with Artichokes, Feta, and Pine Nuts

SERVES 4   TOTAL TIME: 20 MINUTES

4 ounces marinated feta in oil, crumbled (1 cup), plus 2 tablespoons feta oil

2 teaspoons grated lemon zest plus 4 teaspoons juice

1½ pounds spiralized zucchini noodles, cut into 6-inch lengths, divided

2 cups jarred artichoke hearts packed in water, drained, patted dry, and chopped coarse, divided

¼ cup pine nuts or chopped walnuts, toasted

STAPLE INGREDIENTS:

Extra-virgin olive oil
Table salt
Pepper

1. Whisk feta oil, lemon zest and juice, ¼ teaspoon salt, and ¼ teaspoon pepper together in large bowl; set aside.

2. Heat 1 tablespoon olive oil in 12-inch nonstick skillet over high heat until shimmering. Add half of zucchini noodles, half of artichoke hearts, ⅛ teaspoon salt, and ⅛ teaspoon pepper and cook, tossing frequently, until noodles are crisp-tender, 1 to 2 minutes. Transfer to bowl with lemon vinaigrette and toss gently to combine.

3. Add 1 tablespoon oil to now-empty skillet and heat over high heat until shimmering. Add remaining noodles, remaining artichoke hearts, ⅛ teaspoon salt, and ⅛ teaspoon pepper and cook, tossing frequently, until noodles are crisp-tender. Add to zucchini noodle mixture in bowl and toss to coat. Divide among individual serving plates and sprinkle with feta and pine nuts. Serve immediately.

YOU CAN SERVE WITH
CRUSTY BREAD

YOU CAN SERVE WITH

A SIMPLE SALAD

Whether you're meal prepping for yourself or feeding a family, a frittata is a great meal for any time of the day (what is it about eggs that seem simultaneously elegant and low-key?). Everything starts on the stovetop here, with sautéed broccoli and a quick hit of lemon zest and juice kicking things off. Eggs and tangy, herbed goat cheese (or plain if you can't find it) join the party, partially cooking until a spatula leaves a trail in the curds, and then gently finishing in the oven. I like rounding things out with a salad and a white wine spritzer for an elevated take on breakfast for dinner.

—CARMEN DONGO, *Test Cook*

Broccoli and Goat Cheese Frittata

SERVES 4 TO 6 COOKING TIME: 30 MINUTES

12 large eggs

¼ cup whole milk

12 ounces broccoli florets, cut into ½-inch pieces

½ teaspoon grated lemon zest plus ½ teaspoon juice

4 ounces herbed goat cheese, crumbled (1 cup)

STAPLE INGREDIENTS:

Extra-virgin olive oil
Table salt

---

1. Adjust oven rack to middle position and heat oven to 350 degrees. Whisk eggs, milk, and ¼ teaspoon salt together in bowl until well combined.

2. Heat 1 tablespoon olive oil in 12-inch ovensafe nonstick skillet over medium-high heat until shimmering. Add broccoli and ¼ teaspoon salt and cook, stirring frequently, until broccoli is crisp-tender and spotty brown, 4 to 6 minutes. Add 3 tablespoons water and lemon zest and juice and cook, stirring constantly, until broccoli is just tender and skillet is dry, about 1 minute.

3. Add goat cheese and egg mixture to skillet and cook, using rubber spatula to stir and scrape bottom of skillet, until large curds form and spatula leaves trail through eggs but eggs are still very wet, 30 seconds. Smooth curds into even layer and cook, without stirring, for 30 seconds. Transfer skillet to oven and bake until frittata is slightly puffy and surface bounces back when lightly pressed, 6 to 9 minutes. Using rubber spatula, loosen frittata from skillet and transfer to cutting board. Let sit for 5 minutes before slicing and serving.

To pack as much flavor as possible into this cruciferous vegetable (which I always seem to have rolling around in my crisper drawer), I cut a head of cabbage into wedges, brush the wedges with a curry powder–infused oil, and roast them until the edges are charred and crispy with tender, sweet layers underneath. This ensures there are plenty of nooks and crannies exposed, perfect for soaking up a saucy, curried chickpea-tomato mixture that I cook on the stovetop while the wedges are in the oven.

—LEAH COLINS, *Test Cook*

Curried Roasted Cabbage with Chickpeas

SERVES 4   TOTAL TIME: 35 MINUTES

1   tablespoon curry powder, divided

1   head green cabbage (2 pounds), cut through core into eight 2-inch-wide wedges

2   (15-ounce) cans chickpeas, undrained

10 ounces cherry or grape tomatoes, halved

½   cup chopped fresh cilantro

STAPLE INGREDIENTS:

Vegetable oil
Table salt
Pepper

1. Adjust oven rack to lowest position and heat oven to 500 degrees. Combine 2 teaspoons curry powder, 1 teaspoon salt, ¼ teaspoon pepper, and ¼ cup vegetable oil in small bowl. Arrange cabbage wedges in single layer on rimmed baking sheet, then brush cabbage all over with oil mixture. Cover tightly with aluminum foil and roast for 10 minutes. Remove foil and drizzle 2 tablespoons oil evenly over wedges. Return cabbage to oven and roast, uncovered, until cabbage is tender and sides touching sheet are well browned, 12 to 15 minutes.

2. Meanwhile, heat 1 tablespoon oil in 12-inch skillet over medium-high heat until shimmering. Add remaining 1 teaspoon curry powder and cook until fragrant, about 30 seconds. Add chickpeas and their liquid and tomatoes and bring to simmer. Cook, stirring frequently, until tomatoes begin to break down and mixture has thickened slightly, 7 to 10 minutes. Off heat, stir in cilantro.

3. Divide cabbage among individual plates and spoon chickpea mixture over servings. Serve.

To elevate some 'taters to entrée status, I start with sweet potatoes, which are a little heartier than your standard starchy russets. I microwave them, scoop out the tasty insides, and pop the shells in the oven. The reserved sweet potatoes get mashed up with cheddar cheese and chipotle chiles in adobo sauce (use more or less depending on how spicy you like things). Once the shells are a little crispy, I layer in black beans and scallions, then dollop the cheesy mashed sweet potatoes on top. A final sprinkle of more ooey-gooey cheese adds richness and keeps the filling from drying out.

—RUSSELL SELANDER, *Test Cook*

Loaded Sweet Potatoes

SERVES 4 TO 6   TOTAL TIME: 1 HOUR

4   small sweet potatoes (8 ounces each), unpeeled, lightly pricked all over with fork

6   ounces cheddar cheese, shredded (1½ cups), divided

1–2   tablespoons minced canned chipotle chile in adobo sauce

1   (15-ounce) can black beans, rinsed

3   scallions, white parts minced, green parts sliced thin

STAPLE INGREDIENTS:

Extra-virgin olive oil
Table salt

1. Adjust oven rack to middle position and heat oven to 425 degrees. Microwave potatoes on large plate, flipping every 3 minutes, until paring knife glides easily through flesh, 9 to 12 minutes. Let potatoes cool for 5 minutes.

2. Halve each potato lengthwise. Using spoon, scoop flesh from each potato half into medium bowl, leaving about ⅛–¼-inch thickness of flesh; set aside. Place shells cut side up on wire rack set in rimmed baking sheet and bake until dry and slightly crispy, about 10 minutes.

3. Meanwhile, mash reserved potato flesh with potato masher until smooth. Stir in ¾ cup cheddar, chipotle, and ¼ teaspoon salt until well combined. Season with salt and pepper to taste.

4. Toss beans with 1 tablespoon olive oil and scallion whites then divide evenly among parbaked shells. Top with mashed potato mixture and sprinkle with remaining ¾ cup cheddar. Return filled potatoes to rack in baking sheet and bake until spotty brown and warmed through, about 20 minutes. Sprinkle with scallion greens. Serve.

I love toad-in-a-hole, an egg cooked in the hole cut out of a piece of bread, so I turned that concept into a full sheet-pan meal. But instead of the bread, I made hash browns and added kimchi to kick things up a notch. I baked shredded potatoes in the oven on a greased rimmed baking sheet until it was crispy on one side. Then I flipped the potatoes, sprinkled on some kimchi, and made six small indentations in the potatoes to crack eggs into. A quick stint back in the oven and I had perfectly cooked sunny-side up eggs (no making eggs to order!). You will need vegetable oil spray for this recipe.

—RUSSELL SELANDER, *Test Cook*

Toad-in-a-Hole Sheet-Pan Kimchi Hash Browns

SERVES 4 TO 6   TOTAL TIME: 1 HOUR

3 pounds Yukon Gold potatoes, unpeeled

2 scallions, sliced thin

1½ cups kimchi, drained, squeezed dry, and chopped

6 large eggs

2 tablespoons chopped fresh cilantro

STAPLE INGREDIENTS:

Vegetable oil
Table salt
Pepper

1. Adjust oven rack to middle position and heat oven to 450 degrees. Spray rimmed baking sheet with vegetable oil spray. Shred potatoes with food processor or box grater then transfer to large bowl. Cover with cold water and let sit for 5 minutes. Drain potatoes in colander and rinse and dry bowl. Using clean dish towel, squeeze potatoes dry in four batches, transferring dried potatoes to dry, now-empty bowl.

2. Add scallions, ¼ cup vegetable oil, 1 teaspoon salt, and ½ teaspoon pepper to potatoes and toss to combine. Distribute potatoes in even layer on sheet, but do not pack down. Bake until top of potatoes is spotty brown, 32 to 35 minutes.

3. Remove sheet from oven. Using metal spatula, flip hash browns in sections then sprinkle kimchi evenly over top. Using back of spoon, create six 3-inch-wide indentations in potatoes. Crack 1 egg into each and sprinkle with ¼ teaspoon salt and ¼ teaspoon pepper.

4. Bake, rotating sheet halfway through, until whites are just beginning to set but still have some movement when sheet is shaken, 7 to 8 minutes for slightly runny yolks or 9 to 10 minutes for soft-cooked yolks. Season with salt and pepper to taste and sprinkle with cilantro. Serve.

YOU CAN SERVE WITH
A SIMPLE SALAD

In my eyes, there's absolutely no better pairing than potatoes and rosemary, and this unexpected pizza puts that perfect marriage at the forefront. Add caramelized red onions and creamy, tangy bites of goat cheese and you've got yourself something far from your standard pizzeria pie. If you don't have a pizza peel, you can use a parchment-lined rimless or inverted baking sheet to transfer the pizza to the stone. No baking stone? No worries. A preheated rimless or inverted baking sheet works just fine. You'll need some flour to roll out the dough.

—BRENNA DONOVAN, *Editor*

Potato and Onion Pizza with Rosemary and Goat Cheese

SERVES 4   TOTAL TIME: 1 HOUR 10 MINUTES

1   pound pizza dough, room temperature, split into 2 pieces

2   pounds onions, halved and sliced ¼ inch thick

1   pound small red potatoes, unpeeled and sliced very thin

4   ounces goat cheese, crumbled (1 cup), divided

½   teaspoon minced fresh rosemary, divided

STAPLE INGREDIENTS:

Extra-virgin olive oil
Table salt
Pepper

1. Cover dough pieces loosely with plastic wrap. Adjust oven rack to lower-middle position, place baking stone on rack, and heat oven to 500 degrees. Heat 2 tablespoons olive oil in 12-inch nonstick skillet over medium-low heat until shimmering. Stir in onions and ½ teaspoon salt. Cover and cook, stirring occasionally, until onions are softened and have released their juices, about 10 minutes.

2. Remove lid, increase heat to medium-high, and continue to cook, stirring often, until onions are deeply browned, 10 to 15 minutes. Meanwhile, microwave potatoes and 1 tablespoon water in covered bowl until potatoes are just tender, 3 to 7 minutes. Set potatoes aside to cool.

3. Working with 1 piece of dough at a time (keep other piece covered) on lightly floured counter, press and roll dough to form 14 by 8-inch oval. Transfer dough to well-floured pizza peel and reshape as needed. Gently dimple surface of dough with your fingertips. Brush dough liberally with oil. Scatter half of caramelized onions, half of potatoes, ½ cup goat cheese, and ¼ teaspoon rosemary evenly over dough, leaving ½-inch border around edge.

4. Slide pizza carefully onto baking stone and bake until deep golden brown, about 10 minutes, rotating pizza halfway through baking. (Prepare second pizza while first bakes.) Transfer pizza to cutting board and let rest for 5 minutes before slicing and serving. Repeat with remaining dough and toppings, letting stone reheat for 5 minutes before baking second pizza.

Between the flaky puff pastry and creamy, cheesy base, this tart makes eating your vegetables feel like a treat. Boursin cheese anchors the topping as well as adding herby, garlicky flavor. Make sure the Boursin is room temperature, otherwise you could tear the tart dough when trying to spread it over the base. It may look like a lot of filling before the tart goes in the oven, but like magic, the puff will rise around it. To thaw frozen puff pastry, let it sit either in the refrigerator for 24 hours or on the counter for 30 minutes to 1 hour before using. You'll need a light dusting of flour to roll out the dough.

—STEPHANIE PIXLEY, *Editor*

Rustic Butternut Squash and Spinach Tart

SERVES 4   TOTAL TIME: 1 HOUR

1   (5.2-ounce) package Boursin Garlic & Fine Herbs cheese, room temperature

6   ounces (6 cups) baby spinach

1   pound butternut squash, peeled and cut into ½-inch pieces (3 cups)

4   shallots, sliced thin

1   (9½ by 9-inch) sheet puff pastry, thawed

STAPLE INGREDIENTS:

Extra-virgin olive oil
Table salt
Pepper

1. Adjust oven rack to upper-middle position and heat oven to 425 degrees. Line rimmed baking sheet with parchment paper. Combine 1 tablespoon olive oil and Boursin in small bowl; set aside. Microwave spinach and ¼ cup water in covered bowl until spinach is wilted and decreased in volume by half, 3 to 4 minutes. Set aside for 1 minute then drain spinach in colander, pressing with rubber spatula to release liquid. Chop coarsely, then drain and press again; set aside. Microwave squash in now-empty bowl, covered, until just tender, about 8 minutes; drain if needed.

2. Meanwhile, heat 2 tablespoons oil in 12-inch nonstick skillet over medium heat until shimmering. Add shallots, 1 teaspoon pepper, and ½ teaspoon salt and cook, stirring frequently, until well browned and softened, 8 to 10 minutes. Toss shallots, butternut squash, and reserved spinach together in bowl until well combined; set aside.

3. Unfold pastry onto lightly floured counter and roll into 10-inch square; transfer to prepared sheet. Lightly brush outer ½-inch border along edges of pastry with water then fold edges of pastry over by ½ inch, pressing gently to seal. Spread reserved Boursin mixture evenly over dough, avoiding folded border, then spread butternut squash mixture in even layer over top.

4. Bake until pastry is well browned, 20 to 30 minutes, rotating sheet halfway through baking. Transfer sheet to cooling rack and let cool for 10 minutes. Slice and serve warm or at room temperature.

YOU CAN SERVE WITH
A SIMPLE SALAD

YOU CAN SERVE WITH
A SIMPLE SALAD

There's nothing better than a full meal all in one neat and tidy package (and one that you can eat with your hands). These calzones start with store-bought pizza dough and are jam-packed with garlicky broccoli and oozy cheese. There's the traditional mozzarella for that classic ready-for-its-closeup cheesy pull and feta for a salty bite. Be sure to start with room temperature dough, or it'll spring back when you try to roll it out. You'll need a light dusting of flour to roll out the dough.

—BRENNA DONOVAN, *Editor*

Cheesy Broccoli Calzones

SERVES 4   TOTAL TIME: 55 MINUTES

1 pound pizza dough, room temperature, split into 4 pieces

12 ounces broccoli florets, cut into 1-inch pieces

2 cloves garlic, minced

12 ounces mozzarella cheese, shredded (3 cups)

4 ounces feta cheese, crumbled (1 cup)

STAPLE INGREDIENTS:

Extra-virgin olive oil
Table salt

1. Adjust oven rack to middle position and heat oven to 475 degrees. Line rimmed baking sheet with aluminum foil and brush foil with 1 tablespoon olive oil. Place 1 dough piece on clean counter and, using your cupped hand, drag in small circles until dough feels taut and round. Repeat with remaining dough pieces and cover loosely with plastic wrap.

2. Heat 1 tablespoon oil in 12-inch nonstick skillet over medium-high heat until shimmering. Add broccoli and ¼ teaspoon salt and cook, stirring frequently, until broccoli is crisp-tender and well browned, 4 to 6 minutes. Add 3 tablespoons water and garlic and cook, stirring constantly, until broccoli is just tender, about 1 minute longer. Set aside to cool.

3. Working on lightly floured counter, press and roll 1 piece of reserved dough (keep remaining pieces covered) into 8-inch round of even thickness. Repeat with remaining dough pieces. Working with 1 dough round at a time (keep remaining pieces covered), spread one quarter of mozzarella, one quarter of feta, and one quarter of broccoli evenly over half of dough round, leaving 1-inch border at edge. Fold top half of dough over filling and crimp edges to seal. Gently transfer to prepared sheet and repeat with remaining dough rounds and filling.

4. Using sharp knife, cut two 1-inch steam vents on top of each calzone, then brush tops evenly with 1 tablespoon oil. Bake until golden brown, 18 to 22 minutes, rotating sheet halfway through baking. Transfer sheet to wire rack and let calzones cool for 5 minutes. Serve.

Some of my favorite comfort foods happen to be vegetarian, and enchiladas top the list. I especially love this version for its shortcut-embracing procedure that doesn't cut corners in the flavor department. Pepper Jack cheese brings a little heat, and canned pinto beans and meaty mushrooms add heartiness and bulk things up. Using canned enchilada sauce instead of homemade means this dinner is even more low-prep (and in my opinion just as delicious).

—STEPHANIE PIXLEY, *Editor*

Mushroom and Pinto Bean Enchiladas

SERVES 4   TOTAL TIME: 1 HOUR

1   pound white mushrooms, trimmed and sliced thin

1   (15-ounce) can pinto beans, rinsed, divided

8   ounces pepper Jack or Colby Jack cheese, shredded (2 cups), divided

1   (20-ounce) can red enchilada sauce, divided

12 (6-inch) corn tortillas

STAPLE INGREDIENTS:

Vegetable oil
Table salt
Pepper

1. Adjust oven rack to middle position and heat oven to 450 degrees. Heat 2 tablespoons vegetable oil in 12-inch nonstick skillet over medium-high heat until shimmering. Add mushrooms, ½ teaspoon salt, and ½ teaspoon pepper, cover, and cook, stirring occasionally, until mushrooms have released their liquid, 8 to 10 minutes. Remove lid and continue to cook, stirring occasionally, until mushrooms are deep golden brown, 8 to 10 minutes. Remove from heat.

2. Using potato masher, coarsely mash half of beans in large bowl. Stir in mushrooms, ½ cup cheese, ¼ cup sauce, and remaining whole beans and season with salt and pepper to taste.

3. Spread ½ cup sauce over bottom of 13 by 9-inch baking dish. Brush both sides of tortillas with oil then stack tortillas, wrap in damp dish towel, and microwave until warm and pliable, about 1 minute. Working with 1 warm tortilla at a time, spread scant ¼ cup mushroom filling across center. Roll tortilla tightly around filling and place seam side down in dish, arranging enchiladas in 2 columns across width of dish. Cover completely with remaining sauce and sprinkle with remaining 1½ cups cheese.

4. Cover dish tightly with greased aluminum foil and bake until enchiladas are heated through and cheese is melted, 15 to 25 minutes. Let enchiladas cool for 5 minutes. Serve.

YOU CAN SERVE WITH

**RICE OR A
SIMPLE SALAD**

Molletes, open-faced sandwiches with a thick layer of refried beans, melted cheese, and fresh salsa, are a popular breakfast in Mexico City, but I think they're so delicious, I eat them any time of the day. The salty, fatty, creamy combo of refried beans and melted cheese paired with the bright, slightly-acidic fresh tomato topping has an undeniable satiating appeal. In Mexico, individual bolillos are commonly used, but a loaf of French or Italian bread works as well. The most important part is hollowing out the loaf and toasting it—this prevents any sogginess, and keeps things nice and tidy, ensuring all those tasty fillings don't tumble out.

—LEAH COLINS, *Test Cook*

Refried Bean and Cheese Melts

SERVES 4 TO 6   TOTAL TIME: 25 MINUTES

1   (16-inch) loaf French or Italian bread

1   (15-ounce) can refried beans

3   scallions, white and green parts separated and sliced thin

8   ounces pepper Jack cheese, mild cheddar cheese, or Chihuahua cheese, shredded (2 cups)

2   tomatoes, cored and chopped

STAPLE INGREDIENT:

Unsalted butter

1. Soften 4 tablespoons butter; set aside. Adjust oven rack to middle position and heat oven to 400 degrees. Line rimmed baking sheet with aluminum foil. Slice bread in half horizontally, then remove and discard all but ¼ inch of interior crumb. Spread softened butter evenly inside hollowed bread and place cut side up on prepared sheet. Bake until lightly toasted and browned, about 8 minutes.

2. Combine refried beans and scallion whites in bowl. Spread refried bean mixture evenly inside toasted bread and top with cheese. Bake until cheese is just melted, 5 to 7 minutes. Transfer bread to cutting board and top with tomatoes and scallion greens. Slice crosswise into 2-inch lengths and serve warm.

YOU CAN SERVE WITH
A SIMPLE SALAD

Dinner off the Grill

Let's Get Grilling

If you're looking to add big-time flavor without too many extra ingredients, it's time to take it outside. Cooking over fire adds smoky, charred, and savory flavors that change the entire flavor profile of a dish. Plus, it's a great way to keep your kitchen cool in the warmer months. Whether it's chicken, a rack of ribs, or even pizza, everything really is better on the grill. Read on for the two grill setups we use in this book, and some best practices to ensure success.

IF USING GAS

1. Start by making sure you have enough propane in the tank. If your grill doesn't have a gas gauge or tank scale, pour boiling water over the side of the tank. Then, place your hand on the tank. If the water warms the tank, that means the tank is empty. If the tank remains cool to touch, then there is enough fuel inside.

2. Open the lid, turn the burners to high, and ignite. Once your grill is lit, cover it and let it heat for about 15 minutes. Most grills reach their maximum heat level within 15 minutes, but you may need to give yours a few extra minutes on a cold or windy day.

3A. If the recipe says "hot fire" Leave all burners on high.

3B. If the recipe says "medium fire" Turn all burners to medium.

IF USING CHARCOAL

1. Remove cooking grate from grill and open bottom vent completely. Fill the bottom section of chimney starter with crumpled newspaper and set starter on charcoal rack.

2A. If the recipe says "hot fire" Fill chimney starter with charcoal briquettes (6 quarts). Ignite newspaper.

2B. If the recipe says "medium fire" Fill chimney starter halfway with charcoal briquettes (3 quarts). Ignite newspaper.

3. Allow charcoal to burn until briquettes on top are partially covered with ash. Carefully pour briquettes evenly over grill.

4. Set cooking grate in place.

5. Cover, and open lid vent completely. Heat grill until hot, about 5 minutes.

CLEAN YOUR GRILL GRATES

A clean, gunk-free grill grate is key to aggravation-free grilling. (You wouldn't cook in a dirty pan, would you?) Take these small steps every time before grilling and your steaks will never stick to the grates again. *Note:* When grilling fish, it's important to repeat this process until the grate is black and glossy.

1. After you've heated the grill, scrape the grill grate clean with a grill brush.

2. Grab a dish towel (or large wad of paper towels) with tongs, dip it in vegetable oil, and wipe the grill grates thoroughly.

TIPS FOR STAYING ORGANIZED

Perfect Prep

Things move fast once you're cooking over an open flame. Make sure all of your ingredients have been prepped (including cutting your vegetables or protein, as well as making your sauce or vinaigrette) so you're ready to go once you head out the door. Take a tip from restaurant chefs: Use a rimmed baking sheet to organize the various elements of your dish that you'll need at the grill. And to cut down on dishes, you can also use the same rimmed baking sheet to carry the cooked food back inside (as long as there wasn't any raw meat on it).

Take the Temp

You might be tempted to cut into your meat to check the doneness right when it comes off the grill, but put that knife down. Doing so will disrupt the resting time and leave you with a liquidy mess (and you want all those juices to stay inside!). Instead, reach for an instant-read thermometer—it's the simplest way to ensure your meat has finished cooking. Look for one with a wide temperature range (at least -10 to 425 degrees) and a long stem (at least 4 inches) to reach the center of larger cuts.

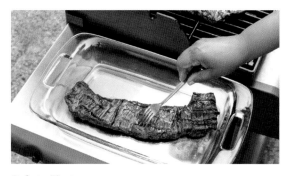

Safety First

Use separate platters (or rimmed baking sheets) for raw and cooked foods, dispose of extra marinade, and apply sauces to meat after it's done cooking to keep your basting brush from becoming contaminated by uncooked meat.

Get Hands-On

When we say "grill over a hot fire," that means the grill should be between 350 to 400 degrees. For "medium," we're aiming for 250 to 300 degrees. But what if your grill doesn't have a temperature gauge? Hold your hand about 5 inches above the preheated cooking grate. If you can leave it there for only 2 seconds, that's hot. Five to 6 seconds is medium.

Whether it's crunchy croutons in a Caesar or crispy shards of pita in fattoush, bread in a salad is a plus in my book. This grilled take on panzanella—a bread-based salad from Tuscany—is no exception. The grill's direct heat creates toasty hunks of bread, the perfect contrast for grilled red peppers and succulent chunks of chicken. Tossing chopped tomatoes with salt draws out their juices, which I mix with store-bought pesto for a simple but flavorful dressing.

—CAMILA CHAPARRO, *Test Cook*

Grilled Bread Salad with Chicken and Bell Peppers

SERVES 4   TOTAL TIME: 40 MINUTES   GRILL HEAT: HOT FIRE

3 tomatoes, cored and cut into ¾-inch pieces

½ cup plus 2 tablespoons pesto

1 12-inch baguette, sliced on bias 1 inch thick

2 red bell peppers, stemmed, seeded, and halved so peppers lay flat

4 (6- to 8-ounce) boneless, skinless chicken breasts, trimmed and pounded to ½-inch thickness

STAPLE INGREDIENTS:

Extra-virgin olive oil
Table salt
Pepper

1. Toss tomatoes with ¼ teaspoon salt in colander set in large bowl and let sit for 30 minutes, tossing occasionally. Measure out ¼ cup tomato juice (if you have less than ¼ cup tomato juice, add red or white wine vinegar to make ¼ cup) then combine with pesto in bowl; set aside.

2. Meanwhile, brush baguette slices and bell peppers with 3 tablespoons olive oil and sprinkle with ¼ teaspoon salt and ⅛ teaspoon pepper. Pat chicken dry with paper towels, rub all over with 1 tablespoon oil, and sprinkle with ½ teaspoon salt and ¼ teaspoon pepper.

3. Grill bell peppers and chicken over hot fire (covered if using gas) until peppers are charred and tender and chicken registers 160 degrees, 10 to 14 minutes, flipping as needed; transfer to cutting board and tent loosely with aluminum foil. Grill bread until lightly charred, 1 to 2 minutes per side; add to cutting board with chicken and peppers.

4. Cut grilled peppers, bread, and chicken into ¾-inch pieces and transfer to serving bowl. Add drained tomatoes and ⅔ cup reserved pesto mixture and toss to combine. Season with salt and pepper to taste, and serve, passing remaining pesto mixture separately.

When I'm stuck on how to make a simple dish vibrant and interesting, I think about contrasts in flavor and texture. In this quick grilled dinner, mildly bitter endive stays on the grill just long enough to wilt the outer layers but retains its signature interior crunch; grassy asparagus spears are charred to contrast with juicy chicken; and bright lemon zest offsets licorice-y tarragon in a twist on the citrus-herb sprinkle, gremolata. Then it's all brought together with a final squeeze of zingy lemon.

—CAMILA CHAPARRO, *Test Cook*

Grilled Chicken, Asparagus, and Endive with Gremolata

SERVES 4   TOTAL TIME: 30 MINUTES   GRILL HEAT: HOT FIRE

2   tablespoons minced fresh tarragon or dill

1   tablespoon grated lemon zest, divided, plus lemon wedges for serving

1   pound asparagus, trimmed

4   heads Belgian endive (4 ounces each), halved lengthwise

4   (6- to 8-ounce) boneless, skinless chicken breasts, trimmed and pounded to ½-inch thickness

STAPLE INGREDIENTS:

Extra-virgin olive oil
Table salt
Pepper

1. Combine tarragon and 2 teaspoons lemon zest in bowl; set gremolata aside until ready to serve.

2. Toss asparagus with 2 tablespoons olive oil, ⅛ teaspoon salt, and pinch pepper in bowl. Toss endive with 1 tablespoon oil, ⅛ teaspoon salt, and pinch pepper in second bowl. Pat chicken dry with paper towels, rub all over with 1 tablespoon oil, and sprinkle with ½ teaspoon salt, ¼ teaspoon pepper, and remaining 1 teaspoon lemon zest.

3. Grill chicken over hot fire (covered if using gas) until well browned and registers 160 degrees, 10 to 14 minutes, flipping as needed. Transfer chicken to serving platter, tent loosely with aluminum foil, and let rest while grilling vegetables.

4. Add asparagus and endive to now-empty grill and grill (covered if using gas) until well browned and crisp-tender, 4 to 10 minutes, flipping as needed. Transfer vegetables to platter with chicken. Sprinkle with gremolata and serve with lemon wedges.

Your first instinct when firing up the grill might not be to reach for tomatoes, but a smoky grill transforms these late-summer beauties into so much more than a sandwich layer. The grill brings the tomatoes' juice to the surface, creating a top-notch saucy situation once they're cut into. Make sure your tomatoes are ripe yet firm so they hold their shape. Sweet-tangy mango chutney spread over the just-off-the-grill chicken mingles with the juicy tomatoes, while warm garam masala–sprinkled naan is the ideal vehicle for scooping up every last bit of sauce.

—SAM BLOCK, *Test Cook*

Grilled Garam Masala Chicken, Tomatoes, and Naan with Chutney

SERVES 4   TOTAL TIME: 50 MINUTES   GRILL HEAT: HOT FIRE

2   pounds ripe but firm tomatoes, cored and halved along equator

4   naan breads

2   teaspoons plus 1 tablespoon garam masala, divided

4   (6- to 8-ounce) boneless, skinless chicken breasts, trimmed and pounded to ½-inch thickness

¼   cup mango chutney, plus extra for serving

STAPLE INGREDIENTS:

Extra-virgin olive oil
Table salt
Pepper

1. Toss tomatoes with 1 tablespoon olive oil, ½ teaspoon salt, and ¼ teaspoon pepper in bowl. Let sit for at least 15 minutes or up to 1 hour.

2. Meanwhile, brush naan with 2 tablespoons oil and sprinkle with 2 teaspoons garam masala. Pat chicken dry with paper towels, rub all over with 1 tablespoon oil, and sprinkle with ½ teaspoon salt, ¼ teaspoon pepper, and remaining 1 tablespoon garam masala.

3. Grill chicken over hot fire (covered if using gas) until well browned and registers 160 degrees, 10 to 14 minutes, flipping as needed. Transfer chicken to serving platter and top with mango chutney. Tent loosely with aluminum foil and let rest while grilling tomatoes and naan.

4. Add tomatoes, cut sides down, to now-empty grill and grill (covered if using gas) until tomatoes are charred, beginning to soften, and juices bubble, 4 to 6 minutes per side. Transfer tomatoes to platter with chicken.

5. Add naan to again-empty grill and grill until lightly charred, about 1 minute per side. Serve chicken, tomatoes, and naan with extra mango chutney.

We've all had our fair share of roasted butternut squash, and for good reason—it's delicious. But if you've never grilled it, you're missing out: Squash is fantastic with a bit of char. Half-inch-thick slices are easy to maneuver on the grill, and they cook through in the time it takes for skewers of curry paste–rubbed chicken to get perfectly browned. A drizzle of bright cilantro-lime vinaigrette offsets the sweet squash, and is the only finishing touch you'll need.

—CAMILA CHAPARRO, *Test Cook*

Grilled Chicken Kebabs with Butternut Squash and Cilantro Vinaigrette

SERVES 4　　　TOTAL TIME: 35 MINUTES　　　GRILL HEAT: MEDIUM FIRE

- 2　tablespoons Thai red or green curry paste

- 2　teaspoons grated lime zest, divided, plus 2 tablespoons juice

- 1½　pounds boneless, skinless chicken thighs, trimmed and cut into 1½-inch pieces

- 2　pounds butternut squash, peeled, halved lengthwise, seeded, and sliced crosswise ½ inch thick

- 2　cups fresh cilantro leaves

STAPLE INGREDIENTS:

Vegetable oil
Table salt
Pepper

---

1. Whisk 2 tablespoons vegetable oil, curry paste, 1 teaspoon lime zest, ½ teaspoon salt, and ¼ teaspoon pepper together in large bowl. Add chicken and toss to coat. Thread chicken onto four 12-inch metal skewers. Toss squash with 2 tablespoons oil, ¼ teaspoon salt, and ⅛ teaspoon pepper in second bowl.

2. Grill chicken kebabs and squash over medium fire (covered if using gas) until well browned and cooked through, 16 to 18 minutes, flipping as needed. Transfer kebabs and squash to serving platter, tent loosely with aluminum foil, and let rest while making vinaigrette.

3. Pulse cilantro, remaining 1 teaspoon lime zest, lime juice, ¼ cup oil, and ¼ teaspoon salt in food processor until cilantro is finely chopped, 6 to 8 pulses, scraping down sides of bowl as needed. Serve chicken and squash with cilantro vinaigrette.

This dish is the Extreme Makeover: Meat and Potatoes Edition. Planks of sweet potatoes grill up beautifully, enhancing their natural sweetness, not to mention that perfectly crispy skin. And beefy steak tips are fast and flavorful, cooking to medium-rare in under 10 minutes. But the revelation here is the grilled scallions: Leaving the alliums whole gives them more of an identity and makes them feel more like a vegetable instead of a mere garnish. Everything's drizzled with a spicy, aromatic sauce—made from harissa, oil, and lime juice—that you'll want to dunk every last bit of sweet potato in.

—SAM BLOCK, *Test Cook*

Grilled Steak Tips with Sweet Potatoes, Scallions, and Harissa Sauce

SERVES 4   TOTAL TIME: 25 MINUTES   GRILL HEAT: HOT FIRE

¼ cup harissa paste

1 tablespoon grated lime zest plus 4 teaspoons juice, divided

1½ pounds sweet potatoes, unpeeled, sliced lengthwise into ½-inch-thick planks

12 scallions

2 pounds sirloin steak tips, trimmed and cut into 2½-inch pieces

STAPLE INGREDIENTS:

Extra-virgin olive oil
Table salt
Pepper

1. Whisk 3 tablespoons olive oil, harissa, and lime juice together in bowl; set harissa sauce aside until ready to serve. Toss potatoes with 2 tablespoons oil, ½ teaspoon salt, and ¼ teaspoon pepper in bowl. Microwave, covered, until softened, 6 to 8 minutes, stirring halfway through.

2. Toss scallions with 1 tablespoon oil, ⅛ teaspoon salt, and ⅛ teaspoon pepper in bowl. Pat steak tips dry with paper towels and sprinkle with ½ teaspoon salt and ¼ teaspoon pepper.

3. Grill steak tips over hot fire (covered if using gas) until meat registers 120 to 125 degrees (for medium-rare), 8 to 10 minutes, flipping as needed. Transfer steak to serving platter, tent loosely with aluminum foil, and let rest while grilling potatoes and scallions.

4. Add potatoes and scallions to now-empty grill and grill (covered if using gas) until lightly charred, 4 to 8 minutes, flipping as needed. Transfer scallions to platter with steak. Toss grilled sweet potatoes with lime zest and 1 tablespoon oil in bowl until coated, then transfer to platter with steak and scallions. Serve with harissa sauce.

YOU CAN SERVE WITH
A SIMPLE SALAD

Once you make this spicy honey butter, you'll want to slather it on anything you can get your hands on. My personal favorite? Biscuits. But one can't eat biscuits for every meal of the day, so do yourself a favor and grill up some quick-cooking flank steak tonight. While it rests, add halved zucchini to the grill and cook until it's tender and charred. Dollop it all with the compound butter, which provides some spicy-yet-rich contrast to the meaty, savory steak and smoky, delicately sweet zucchini.

—BRENNA DONOVAN, *Editor*

Grilled Flank Steak with Zucchini and Spicy Honey Butter

SERVES 4   TOTAL TIME: 25 MINUTES   GRILL HEAT: HOT FIRE

1   shallot, minced

1   teaspoon honey

½   teaspoon cayenne pepper

4   small zucchini (6 ounces each), halved lengthwise

1   (1½-pound) flank steak, 1 inch thick, trimmed

STAPLE INGREDIENTS:

Vegetable oil
Unsalted butter
Table salt
Pepper

1. Soften 4 tablespoons butter then mash with shallot, honey, and cayenne in bowl until combined; set honey butter aside until ready to serve. Brush zucchini with 2 teaspoons vegetable oil then sprinkle with ½ teaspoon salt and ¼ teaspoon pepper. Pat steak dry with paper towels and sprinkle with ½ teaspoon salt and ¼ teaspoon pepper.

2. Grill steak over hot fire (covered if using gas) until meat registers 120 to 125 degrees (for medium-rare), 8 to 12 minutes, flipping as needed. Transfer to cutting board, tent loosely with aluminum foil, and let rest while zucchini cooks.

3. Add zucchini to now-empty grill and grill (covered if using gas) until tender, 5 to 7 minutes, flipping halfway through; transfer to serving platter. Slice steak thin against grain and transfer to platter with zucchini. Dollop steak and zucchini with reserved honey butter. Serve.

I do not discriminate when it comes to my love of cauliflower—roasted, sautéed, even "riced"—but I really, really love grilled wedges of cauliflower. The secret to getting it cooked through without burning the outside? The microwave! (You saw that coming, right?) This way, the cauliflower is cooked through and just needs a few minutes on the grill to get that nice browning. Fatty skirt steak sprinkled with smoked paprika is the perfect accompaniment, and the chimichurri-inspired parsley vinaigrette contributes an herbaceous zip.

—SAM BLOCK, *Test Cook*

Grilled Skirt Steak and Cauliflower with Parsley Vinaigrette

SERVES 4   TOTAL TIME: 30 MINUTES   GRILL HEAT: HOT FIRE

1   head cauliflower (2 pounds), trimmed and cut through core into 6 wedges

2   cups fresh parsley leaves

2   tablespoons red wine vinegar

1   (1½-pound) skirt steak, trimmed and cut with grain into 4 pieces

2   teaspoons smoked paprika

STAPLE INGREDIENTS:

Extra-virgin olive oil
Table salt
Pepper

1. Toss cauliflower with 2 tablespoons olive oil, ½ teaspoon salt, and ½ teaspoon pepper in bowl. Microwave, covered, until paring knife inserted in thickest part of cauliflower meets little resistance, 8 to 12 minutes, stirring gently halfway through.

2. Meanwhile, pulse parsley, vinegar, ¼ cup oil, and ¼ teaspoon salt in food processor until parsley is finely chopped, 8 to 10 pulses, scraping down sides of bowl as needed; set vinaigrette aside until ready to serve. Pat steaks dry with paper towels and sprinkle with smoked paprika, ½ teaspoon salt, and ½ teaspoon pepper.

3. Grill steaks over hot fire (covered if using gas) until meat registers 120 to 125 degrees (for medium-rare), 4 to 6 minutes, flipping as needed. Transfer steaks to cutting board, tent loosely with aluminum foil, and let rest while grilling cauliflower.

4. Arrange cauliflower cut sides down on now-empty grill and grill (covered if using gas), until well browned on cut sides, 4 to 6 minutes, flipping halfway through. Slice steaks thin against grain. Serve steak with cauliflower and reserved parsley vinaigrette.

YOU CAN SERVE WITH

RICE, QUINOA, OR POLENTA

Here I paid homage to pai huang gua, the Chinese smashed cucumber dish that is a perfect foil to rich food. Smashing cucumbers with a rolling pin both speeds up the salting step (to get rid of excess water) and helps relieve a little tension while you're at it. After the cukes drain, toss the craggy pieces with some rice vinegar and soy sauce, plus pepper flakes for a bit of heat. Melted butter whisked together with more soy sauce and drizzled over some gorgeously marbled strip steaks brings the whole meal together.

—SAM BLOCK, *Test Cook*

Grilled Strip Steaks with Smashed Cucumber Salad

SERVES 4   TOTAL TIME: 30 MINUTES   GRILL HEAT: HOT FIRE

2   tablespoons soy sauce, divided

2   English cucumbers, quartered lengthwise and cut crosswise into 2-inch lengths

2   (1-pound) strip steaks, 1 inch thick, trimmed

2   tablespoons seasoned rice vinegar

½   teaspoon red pepper flakes

STAPLE INGREDIENTS:

Unsalted butter
Table salt
Pepper

1. Melt 4 tablespoons butter then combine with 1 tablespoon soy sauce; set soy butter aside until ready to serve. Combine cucumbers and ½ teaspoon salt in 1-gallon zipper-lock bag, seal bag, and turn to distribute salt. Using rolling pin or small skillet, gently smash cucumbers in bag; set aside.

2. Pat steaks dry with paper towels and sprinkle with ½ teaspoon salt and ½ teaspoon pepper. Grill over hot fire (covered if using gas) until meat registers 120 to 125 degrees (for medium-rare), 8 to 16 minutes, flipping as needed. Transfer steaks to cutting board, tent loosely with aluminum foil, and let rest for 5 minutes.

3. Meanwhile, drain cucumbers in colander. Whisk vinegar, remaining 1 tablespoon soy sauce, and pepper flakes together in large bowl. Add cucumbers and toss to combine; set salad aside until ready to serve.

4. Slice steaks ½ inch thick. Drizzle steaks with reserved soy butter and serve with cucumber salad.

YOU CAN SERVE WITH
RICE

YOU CAN SERVE WITH
A SIMPLE SALAD

Sometimes nothing hits the spot quite like an old-school steakhouse dinner, and strip steak and potatoes topped with a parsley/garlic–spiked compound butter certainly does the trick (albeit without the tufted leather furniture and bow tie–clad servers). Briefly microwaved potatoes turn creamy and charred on the grill and cook in the time it takes for the steaks to rest. The garlic butter melts over the steak, and any extra is soaked up by the hot-off-the-grill potatoes. Now all that's missing is a glass of red wine (might as well make it two—it's on the house).

—BRENNA DONOVAN, *Editor*

Grilled Strip Steaks and Potatoes with Garlic Butter

SERVES 4   TOTAL TIME: 35 MINUTES   GRILL HEAT: HOT FIRE

2   tablespoons minced fresh parsley

3   garlic cloves, minced

1½   pounds small (1- to 2-inch-wide) red or yellow potatoes, halved

2   (1-pound) strip steaks, 1 inch thick, trimmed

STAPLE INGREDIENTS:

Extra-virgin olive oil
Unsalted butter
Table salt
Pepper

1. Soften 4 tablespoons butter then mash with parsley, garlic, ½ teaspoon salt, and ⅛ teaspoon pepper in bowl until combined; set garlic butter aside until ready to serve. Toss potatoes with 1 tablespoon olive oil, ¼ teaspoon salt, and ⅛ teaspoon pepper in bowl. Microwave, covered, until potatoes offer slight resistance when pierced with tip of paring knife, about 6 minutes, stirring halfway through. Drain if necessary, then toss with additional 1 tablespoon oil.

2. Pat steaks dry with paper towels and sprinkle with ½ teaspoon salt and ¼ teaspoon pepper. Grill over hot fire (covered if using gas) until meat registers 120 to 125 degrees (for medium-rare), 8 to 16 minutes, flipping as needed. Transfer steaks to cutting board, dollop with half of reserved garlic butter, tent loosely with aluminum foil, and let rest while grilling potatoes.

3. Add potatoes to now-empty grill and grill (covered if using gas) until potatoes are well browned and tender, 8 to 12 minutes, flipping as needed. Add potatoes to bowl with remaining garlic butter and toss to coat. Slice steaks ½ inch thick. Serve with potatoes.

Grilled dinners that practically cook themselves are my summer go-tos, and this combo of quick-cooking pork tenderloin and a salad of charred juicy peaches, peppery arugula, and tangy goat cheese is as easy as it is tasty. Prep the pork and peaches while the balsamic vinegar reduces, hit the grill, then toss together a quick salad and slice the meat. The peaches are a natural pairing with fruit-friendly pork, and a drizzle of sweet-tart balsamic reduction makes the whole dish feel fancy with hardly any effort.

—CAMILA CHAPARRO, *Test Cook*

Grilled Pork Tenderloin Steaks with Grilled Peach and Arugula Salad

SERVES 4   TOTAL TIME: 30 MINUTES   GRILL HEAT: HOT FIRE

½ cup balsamic vinegar

2 ripe but firm peaches, halved and pitted

2 (12- to 16-ounce) pork tenderloins, trimmed, each pounded to ½-inch thickness and halved crosswise

5 ounces (5 cups) baby arugula

4 ounces herbed goat cheese, crumbled (1 cup)

STAPLE INGREDIENTS:

Extra-virgin olive oil
Table salt
Pepper

1. Bring vinegar to simmer in 12-inch skillet over medium-high heat and cook until syrupy and reduced to scant ¼ cup, about 6 minutes; transfer to bowl and set aside. (Balsamic reduction can be refrigerated for up to 3 days.)

2. Rub peaches all over with 1 teaspoon olive oil and sprinkle with ⅛ teaspoon salt and pinch pepper. Pat pork dry with paper towels, rub all over with 2 teaspoons oil, and sprinkle with ½ teaspoon salt and ¼ teaspoon pepper.

3. Grill peaches over hot fire (covered if using gas) until charred and tender, about 6 minutes, flipping halfway through. Transfer to cutting board. Grill pork (covered if using gas) until lightly charred and meat registers 140 degrees, 4 to 6 minutes, flipping as needed. Transfer to cutting board with peaches, tent loosely with aluminum foil, and let rest while assembling salad.

4. Chop peaches into 1-inch pieces, then toss with arugula, 1 tablespoon olive oil, ⅛ teaspoon salt, and pinch pepper in serving bowl. Sprinkle with goat cheese. Slice pork ½ inch thick and serve with salad and balsamic reduction.

If you've got no patience for prep, bookmark this recipe—leaving pork tenderloins whole when you grill them is about as low-prep as it gets. Thin stalks of broccolini—broccoli's milder, sweeter, and altogether more delicate cousin (no offense, broccoli)—cook quickly as the tenderloins rest. All that's left to do once you bring it all inside is make a toasty, nutty, browned butter with hazelnuts that crisp up in the pan. Chopped fresh basil (added off the heat so it doesn't scorch) brings an herbal note to the whole dish.

—BRENNA DONOVAN, *Editor*

Grilled Pork Tenderloin with Broccolini and Hazelnut Browned Butter

SERVES 4   TOTAL TIME: 40 MINUTES   GRILL HEAT: HOT FIRE

1   **pound broccolini, trimmed and stems halved lengthwise**

2   **(12 to 16-ounce) pork tenderloins, trimmed**

½   **cup blanched hazelnuts, chopped**

3   **tablespoons shredded fresh basil**

1   **tablespoon lemon juice**

STAPLE INGREDIENTS:

Extra-virgin olive oil
Unsalted butter
Table salt
Pepper

---

1. Toss broccolini with 2 tablespoons olive oil, ¼ teaspoon salt, and ¼ teaspoon pepper in bowl. Pat pork dry with paper towels and sprinkle with ½ teaspoon salt and ¼ teaspoon pepper.

2. Grill pork over hot fire (covered if using gas) until lightly charred and meat registers 140 degrees, about 15 minutes, flipping as needed. Transfer to serving platter and tent loosely with aluminum foil and let rest.

3. Meanwhile, add broccolini to now-empty grill and grill (covered if using gas) until charred and tender, 8 to 10 minutes, flipping as needed; transfer to platter with pork.

4. Cook 8 tablespoons butter, hazelnuts, and ¼ teaspoon salt in 10-inch skillet over medium heat until nuts are toasted and butter is lightly browned, about 4 minutes. Remove from heat and stir in basil and lemon juice. Serve pork and broccolini with hazelnut butter.

YOU CAN SERVE WITH

**POLENTA OR
CRUSTY BREAD**

I love pork tenderloin, but I usually associate it with fall comfort food—this recipe helps me shake up my porky routine. Maybe you've caught on by now, but the never-fail equation for an easy, flavor-packed meal on the grill is protein + vegetable + compound butter. Here a salty feta, fresh mint, and orange zest concoction melts over beautifully browned pork and spears of grilled zucchini, turning into a luxurious sauce that falls firmly in warm weather–dinner territory.

—BRENNA DONOVAN, *Editor*

Grilled Pork Cutlets and Zucchini with Feta and Mint Compound Butter

SERVES 4 TO 6   TOTAL TIME: 25 MINUTES   GRILL HEAT: HOT FIRE

1 ounce feta cheese, crumbled (¼ cup)

1 tablespoon chopped fresh mint

½ teaspoon grated orange zest

4 small zucchini (6 ounces each), halved lengthwise

2 (12- to 16-ounce) pork tenderloins, trimmed and cut crosswise into 4 equal pieces

STAPLE INGREDIENTS:

Vegetable oil
Unsalted butter
Table salt
Pepper

1. Soften 4 tablespoons butter then mash with feta, mint, orange zest, ¼ teaspoon salt, and ¼ teaspoon pepper in bowl until combined; set feta butter aside until ready to serve. Rub zucchini all over with 1 tablespoon vegetable oil and sprinkle with ¼ teaspoon salt and ⅛ teaspoon pepper. Stand pork pieces cut sides down on cutting board, cover with plastic wrap, and pound to even ¼-inch thickness. Pat cutlets dry with paper towels and sprinkle with ½ teaspoon salt and ¼ teaspoon pepper.

2. Grill pork over hot fire (covered if using gas) until lightly charred and meat registers 140 degrees, 4 to 6 minutes, flipping as needed. Transfer to serving platter, tent loosely with aluminum foil, and let rest while grilling zucchini.

3. Add zucchini to now-empty grill and grill (covered if using gas) until tender, 5 to 7 minutes, flipping halfway through; transfer to platter with pork. Dollop pork and zucchini with reserved feta butter. Serve.

YOU CAN SERVE WITH

CORNBREAD

If you've never made a rack of ribs, I don't blame you—it's usually an hours-long labor of love. Not anymore. The trick to achieving smoky, fall-off-the-bone ribs in record time is simmering the baby backs in salted water, which tenderizes the meat so there's no need for low and slow once you get grilling. Slathered with your favorite barbecue sauce, the ribs caramelize into a succulent, extra-napkins-needed delight you thought was only possible at your neighborhood smokehouse. Coleslaw with a kick (thanks to pickled jalapeños) balances out the sticky sweetness.

—SAM BLOCK, *Test Cook*

Grilled Ribs with Spicy Slaw

SERVES 4   TOTAL TIME: 1 HOUR   GRILL HEAT: MEDIUM FIRE

1 (14-ounce) bag green coleslaw mix

2 (2-pound) racks baby back ribs, trimmed, membrane removed, and each rack halved crosswise

1 cup barbecue sauce, divided, plus extra for serving

½ cup mayonnaise

¼ cup pickled jalapeños, chopped fine, plus 2 tablespoons brine

STAPLE INGREDIENTS:

Table salt
Pepper

1. Toss coleslaw mix with 1 teaspoon salt in colander set over medium bowl. Let sit until cabbage begins to wilt, about 30 minutes. Rinse coleslaw mix then pat dry with paper towels; set aside. (Rinsed and patted dry coleslaw mix can be refrigerated for up to 24 hours.)

2. Meanwhile, bring 2½ quarts water, ribs, and 2 tablespoons salt to simmer in Dutch oven over high heat. Reduce heat to maintain bare simmer, cover, and cook until thickest part of ribs registers 195 degrees, 15 to 25 minutes.

3. Remove ribs from pot and pat dry with paper towels, then brush ribs all over with ⅓ cup barbecue sauce. Grill ribs over medium fire (covered if using gas) until glaze is caramelized and charred in spots, 15 to 20 minutes, brushing ribs all over with ⅓ cup barbecue sauce halfway through cooking and flipping as needed. Transfer ribs to cutting board, brush all over with remaining ⅓ cup barbecue sauce, tent loosely with aluminum foil, and let rest for 5 minutes.

4. Toss salted coleslaw mix, mayonnaise, pickled jalapenos, and brine together in bowl until evenly coated. Season with salt and pepper to taste. Cut ribs between bones to separate. Serve with coleslaw and extra barbecue sauce.

Grilled corn and grilled shrimp might not be news to you, but have you ever grilled an avocado? Imagine the buttery, grassy flavor you're used to, but crisp and smoky. Lime on the grill is also a slam dunk—it turns into a caramelized element, bringing more nuance to its acidity. Be sure to find avocados that are a little underripe, as they will be easier to handle on the grill. You will need four 12-inch metal skewers for this recipe. I like using jumbo shrimp (16 to 20 per pound) here. Some shrimp are treated with salt or additives like sodium tripolyphosphate (STPP); if using treated shrimp, skip adding salt to the shrimp in step 1.

—SAM BLOCK, *Test Cook*

Grilled Shrimp, Corn, and Avocado Salad

SERVES 4   TOTAL TIME: 35 MINUTES   GRILL HEAT: HOT FIRE

2   avocados, halved and pitted

3   ears corn, husks and
    silk removed

1½ pounds shrimp, peeled
    and deveined

2   teaspoons grated lime zest
    (2 limes), limes halved

3   romaine lettuce hearts
    (6 ounces each), halved
    lengthwise and chopped

STAPLE INGREDIENTS:

Extra-virgin olive oil
Table salt
Pepper

1. Rub cut sides of avocados with 1 teaspoon olive oil. Rub corn all over with 2 teaspoons oil and sprinkle with ½ teaspoon salt and ½ teaspoon pepper. Pat shrimp dry with paper towels then toss with 1 tablespoon oil, ¼ teaspoon salt, and ¼ teaspoon pepper. Thread shrimp tightly onto four 12-inch metal skewers and tightly pack (6 to 8 shrimp per skewer), alternating direction of each shrimp.

2. Grill corn over hot fire (covered if using gas) until charred on all sides, 10 to 13 minutes, turning as needed; transfer to cutting board. Grill avocados and lime halves (covered if using gas), cut sides down, until lightly charred, about 2 minutes; add to cutting board with corn and let cool slightly, about 5 minutes.

3. Meanwhile, grill shrimp (covered if using gas) until lightly charred and opaque throughout, about 2 minutes per side. Using tongs, slide shrimp off skewers into clean bowl and toss with 1 tablespoon oil and lime zest; set aside.

4. Using spoon, scoop avocado flesh from skin and cut into 1-inch pieces. Cut kernels from cob. Juice limes to yield ¼ cup. Whisk lime juice, 3 tablespoons olive oil, ¼ teaspoon salt, and ¼ teaspoon pepper together in large bowl. Add romaine, avocado, corn, and shrimp and toss gently to combine. Season with salt and pepper to taste and serve.

Coleslaw might be famous for its cool and mayo-forward preparation—don't get me wrong, I'm a fan (see page 231)—but making it on the grill turns it into a whole new side dish. Red cabbage has a higher sugar content than green, so it caramelizes beautifully. Balanced with sweet shredded Asian pear and nutty toasted sesame oil, it's the star sidekick to buttery salmon. Using a small head of cabbage is essential, as each wedge needs enough core to hold itself together on the grill. If you can only find a larger head, don't stress; peel away at the leaves of the cabbage until it reaches roughly 1¼ pounds.

—SAM BLOCK, *Test Cook*

Grilled Salmon with Charred Red Cabbage Slaw

SERVES 4   TOTAL TIME: 30 MINUTES   GRILL HEAT: HOT FIRE

1   small head (1¼ pounds) red cabbage, cut through core into 1-inch-wide wedges

4   (6- to 8-ounce) skin-on salmon fillets, 1 inch thick

2   teaspoons grated lime zest (2 limes), limes halved

1   tablespoon toasted sesame oil

1   Asian pear, unpeeled, cored, and shredded

STAPLE INGREDIENTS:

Extra-virgin olive oil
Table salt
Pepper

---

1. Rub cabbage all over with 1 tablespoon olive oil and sprinkle with ¼ teaspoon salt and ¼ teaspoon pepper. Pat salmon dry with paper towels, rub all over with 2 teaspoons olive oil, and sprinkle flesh side with ½ teaspoon salt and ½ teaspoon pepper.

2. Grill cabbage and lime halves over hot fire (covered if using gas) until lightly charred and cabbage is beginning to wilt, 4 to 8 minutes, flipping cabbage halfway through. Transfer to cutting board to cool while grilling salmon.

3. Add salmon to now-empty grill, flesh side down and perpendicular to grate bars. Grill salmon fillets, covered (reducing heat to medium if using gas), and cook until well marked and centers are translucent when checked with tip of paring knife and register 125 degrees (for medium-rare), 4 to 6 minutes per side; transfer to serving platter.

4. Once lime halves and cabbage are cool enough to handle, juice limes to yield ¼ cup and thinly slice cabbage, discarding core. Whisk lime zest and juice, sesame oil, 2 tablespoons olive oil, ¼ teaspoon salt, and ¼ teaspoon pepper together in large bowl. Add sliced cabbage and shredded pear and toss to coat, then season with salt and pepper to taste. Serve with grilled salmon.

YOU CAN SERVE WITH
CRUSTY BREAD

This light, summery, and superflavorful meal couldn't be easier, but the home run here is the crispy capers. If you're anything like me, once you make them you're going to want to put them on everything. Fry them quickly in the microwave until they turn into salty little flavor bombs, and then use the briny frying oil to impart additional caper-y goodness to the veggies. Tucked into a foil packet with cod and lemon slices, this is just as easy to clean up as it is to make.

—SAM BLOCK, *Test Cook*

Grilled Cod and Summer Squash Packets with Crispy Capers

SERVES 4   TOTAL TIME: 35 MINUTES   GRILL HEAT: HOT FIRE

¼ cup capers, rinsed

1 pound yellow summer squash, sliced into ¼-inch-thick rounds

12 ounces plum tomatoes, cored and sliced into ½-inch-thick rounds

4 (6- to 8-ounce) skinless cod fillets, 1 inch thick

1 lemon, sliced into ¼-inch-thick rounds

STAPLE INGREDIENTS:

Extra-virgin olive oil
Table salt
Pepper

1. Microwave capers and ½ cup olive oil in bowl (capers should be mostly submerged) until capers are darkened in color and have shrunk, about 5 minutes, stirring halfway through. Using slotted spoon, transfer capers to paper towel–lined plate (they will continue to crisp as they cool); set aside and reserve oil.

2. Combine caper oil, squash, tomatoes, 1 teaspoon salt, and 1 teaspoon pepper in bowl. Arrange four 18 by 14-inch sheets aluminum foil flat on counter. Divide vegetable mixture evenly among foil sheets. Pat cod dry with paper towels and sprinkle with ¼ teaspoon salt and ¼ teaspoon pepper, place on top of vegetables, then top with lemon slices. Bring short sides of foil together and crimp tightly to seal. Crimp remaining open ends of packets.

3. Grill packets over hot fire (covered if using gas) until cod registers 135 degrees and vegetables are tender, about 10 minutes (insert an instant-read thermometer through the foil into thickest part of fish to test for doneness). Carefully open packets, allowing steam to escape away from you. Using thin metal spatula, gently slide cod, vegetables, and any accumulated juices onto individual plates. Drizzle with olive oil to taste and sprinkle with crispy capers. Serve.

Sometimes all you need to freshen up your meal rotation is a new spin on a familiar ingredient. Instead of grilling swordfish steaks, cube up the mild-flavored firm fish, toss with lemon, oil, and Italian herbs, and thread onto kebabs. And for zucchini, instead of sautéing coins, which can easily overcook and turn to mush, try a salad of crisp, no-cook zucchini ribbons that are quickly tossed with lemon, olive oil, and shaved Parmesan. Shaved zuke feels like an entirely new vegetable, and is my new favorite way to enjoy summer squash. Same ingredients, different stories. You will need four 12-inch metal skewers for this recipe.

—CAMILA CHAPARRO, *Test Cook*

Grilled Swordfish Kebabs with Zucchini Ribbon Salad

SERVES 4   TOTAL TIME: 25 MINUTES   GRILL HEAT: HOT FIRE

1 tablespoon dried Italian seasoning, herbes de Provence, or dried oregano

1½ teaspoons grated lemon zest, divided, plus ¼ cup lemon juice, divided (2 lemons)

2 pounds skinless swordfish steaks, 1 inch thick, cut into 1-inch pieces

3 zucchini (8 ounces each), shaved lengthwise into ribbons

3 ounces Parmesan cheese, shaved

STAPLE INGREDIENTS:

Extra-virgin olive oil
Table salt
Pepper

1. Whisk ¼ cup olive oil, Italian seasoning, 1 teaspoon lemon zest, 2 tablespoons lemon juice, ¾ teaspoon salt, and ¼ teaspoon pepper together in large bowl. Add swordfish and toss to coat. Thread swordfish evenly onto four 12-inch metal skewers.

2. Grill kebabs over hot fire (covered if using gas) until swordfish registers 130 degrees, 8 to 12 minutes, turning as needed. Transfer to platter and tent loosely with aluminum foil while making zucchini salad.

3. Whisk 3 tablespoons olive oil, remaining ½ teaspoon lemon zest, remaining 2 tablespoons lemon juice, ½ teaspoon salt, and ¼ teaspoon pepper together in large bowl. Add zucchini and Parmesan and toss to coat. Serve with swordfish.

During the usual meat-heavy grilling season it's nice to break things up with a vegetable-forward meal, and it doesn't get more veggie-centric than this colorful platter. But far from feeling lean, this hearty offering is full of starchy, creamy potatoes; crisp-tender broccolini; and sweet red peppers. Served with a rich and flavorful pesto and a sprinkle of creamy feta cheese, this is the meal you've been waiting for without even realizing it.

—CAMILA CHAPARRO, *Test Cook*

Grilled Vegetable Platter with Pesto

SERVES 4   TOTAL TIME: 40 MINUTES   GRILL HEAT: MEDIUM FIRE

1½ pounds small (1- to 2-inch wide) red or yellow potatoes, halved

1½ pounds broccolini, trimmed and stems halved lengthwise

3 red bell peppers, stemmed, seeded, and halved so peppers lay flat

4 ounces feta or goat cheese, crumbled (1 cup)

½ cup pesto

STAPLE INGREDIENTS:

Extra-virgin olive oil
Table salt
Pepper

1. Toss potatoes with 1 tablespoon olive oil, ¼ teaspoon salt, and ⅛ teaspoon pepper in bowl. Cover and microwave until potatoes offer slight resistance when pierced with tip of paring knife, about 6 minutes, stirring halfway through. Drain, if necessary, then toss with additional 1 tablespoon oil.

2. Toss broccolini with 2 tablespoons oil, ¼ teaspoon salt, and ⅛ teaspoon pepper. Rub peppers all over with 1 tablespoon oil and sprinkle with ⅛ teaspoon salt and pinch pepper.

3. Grill peppers and potatoes over medium fire (covered if using gas) until well browned and tender, 10 to 12 minutes, flipping as needed. Transfer grilled vegetables to cutting board and tent loosely with aluminum foil. Add broccolini to now-empty grill and grill (covered if using gas) until charred and tender, 8 to 10 minutes, flipping as needed; transfer to cutting board with vegetables.

4. Slice peppers into 1-inch-wide strips then arrange potatoes, sliced peppers, and broccolini on serving platter. Sprinkle with feta and serve with pesto.

Just because summer's winding down, doesn't mean it's time to put away the grill. A hearty autumnal salad of earthy kale, crispy apples, crumbles of garlicky herbal Boursin cheese, and just-spicy-enough pepperoncini is perfectly at home atop grilled pizza dough, where the kale and cheese soften slightly. Grilling pizza dough is also one of the best uses of your grill—it's hotter than your oven, and chars better too. Be sure to let the dough come to room temperature first; it makes it much easier to roll out. You'll need a light dusting of flour to roll out the dough.

—CAMILA CHAPARRO, *Test Cook*

Grilled Flatbread with Kale and Apples

SERVES 4   TOTAL TIME: 40 MINUTES   GRILL HEAT: MEDIUM FIRE

1 pound pizza dough, room temperature, split into 2 pieces

6 ounces kale, stemmed and cut into 1-inch pieces

1 apple, cored, halved, and sliced ¼ inch thick

1 (5.2-ounce) package Boursin Garlic & Fine Herbs cheese, chilled and crumbled (1 cup)

⅓ cup sliced pepperoncini

STAPLE INGREDIENTS:

Extra-virgin olive oil
Table salt
Pepper

1. Cover dough pieces loosely with plastic wrap. Combine kale, 3 tablespoons olive oil, ¼ teaspoon salt, and ⅛ teaspoon pepper in bowl. Vigorously squeeze and massage kale mixture with hands until leaves are uniformly darkened and slightly wilted, about 1 minute. Add apple, Boursin, and pepperoncini and toss to combine; set aside.

2. Line rimmed baking sheet with parchment paper and dust with flour. Working with 1 piece of dough at a time (keep other piece covered) on lightly floured counter, press and roll dough to form 12-inch by 8-inch rectangle. Transfer to prepared sheet, reshaping as needed, sprinkle lightly with flour, and top with second sheet of parchment. Lightly flour second sheet of parchment. Repeat with remaining dough, stacking dough rectangle on floured parchment.

3. Brush top of 1 dough rectangle with 1 tablespoon oil. Grill first dough rectangle, oiled side down, over medium fire until underside is spotty brown and top is covered with bubbles, 2 to 3 minutes (pop any large bubbles that form). Brush top of dough with 1 tablespoon oil, then flip. Scatter half of kale mixture evenly over browned side of flatbread then grill until second side is spotty brown and cheese is softened slightly, 3 to 5 minutes. Transfer to cutting board. Repeat with remaining dough, 2 tablespoons oil, and remaining kale mixture. Cut flatbreads into wedges, drizzle with olive oil to taste, and serve. (You can keep the first flatbread warm on wire rack set inside rimmed baking sheet in 200-degree oven.)

I love every component of this dish, not only for the flavors and textures, but for their efficiency. To begin, microwaved crispy shallots bring a savory onion flavor (and of course irresistible texture) to grilled tofu and broccoli. But here I also use the often-discarded shallot oil to add extra *oomph* to the broccoli, which is grilled to the perfect level of char and crunch. Red curry paste spices up the slabs of tofu, and then helps create a two-ingredient peanut sauce that is way more than the sum of its parts.

—CAMILA CHAPARRO, *Test Cook*

Grilled Tofu with Charred Broccoli and Peanut Sauce

SERVES 4   TOTAL TIME: 40 MINUTES   GRILL HEAT: HOT FIRE

2   (14-ounce) blocks firm tofu, each block sliced lengthwise into 4 slabs

¼   cup creamy peanut butter

5   teaspoons Thai red curry paste, divided

3   shallots, sliced thin

1½ pounds broccoli crowns, cut into 4 wedges if 3 to 4 inches in diameter or 6 wedges if 4 to 5 inches in diameter

---

STAPLE INGREDIENTS:

Vegetable oil
Table salt
Pepper

---

1. Spread tofu slabs over paper towel–lined baking sheet and let drain for 20 minutes.

2. Meanwhile, whisk 5 tablespoons warm water, peanut butter, and 1 teaspoon curry paste in bowl until smooth; set aside until ready to serve. Microwave shallots and ½ cup plus 2 tablespoons vegetable oil in medium bowl for 5 minutes. Stir and continue to microwave in 2-minute increments until beginning to brown (2 to 6 minutes). Repeat stirring and microwaving in 30-second increments until golden brown (30 seconds to 2 minutes). Using slotted spoon, transfer shallots to paper towel–lined plate and season with salt to taste; reserve shallot oil. (You should have about 7 tablespoons reserved oil, if you have less, add vegetable oil to make 7 tablespoons.)

3. Toss broccoli with 5 tablespoons reserved shallot oil, ¼ teaspoon salt, and ⅛ teaspoon pepper in bowl; set aside. Whisk remaining 4 teaspoons curry paste, remaining 2 tablespoons reserved shallot oil, ¼ teaspoon salt, and ⅛ teaspoon pepper together in bowl then brush tofu all over with curry paste mixture.

4. Grill broccoli and tofu over hot fire (covered if using gas) until broccoli is charred in spots and tofu is well browned, 6 to 10 minutes, turning broccoli as needed and gently flipping tofu halfway through cooking. Serve tofu and broccoli with reserved peanut sauce and crispy shallots.

YOU CAN SERVE WITH

RICE

YOU CAN SERVE WITH

**CORNBREAD OR
A SIMPLE SALAD**

Feast your eyes on the meatiest meatless meal around. Tempeh, an ingredient made from fermented soy beans, provides a texture that mimics meat, making it a great alternative. Barbecue sauce plays double-duty, serving both as a sweet and smoky marinade for the tempeh as well as a glaze for the kebabs, so they become caramelized when grilled. Those bags of adorable snackable mini peppers work great as kebabs, leaving the prep list practically effortless. You will need eight 12-inch metal skewers for this recipe.

—SAM BLOCK, *Test Cook*

Grilled Barbecue Tempeh Skewers

SERVES 4   TOTAL TIME: 35 MINUTES   GRILL HEAT: HOT FIRE

1¼ cups barbecue sauce, divided

1 pound tempeh, cut into 1½-inch pieces

1 pound cremini mushrooms, trimmed

1 pound sweet mini peppers, whole, or 2 red bell peppers, stemmed, seeded, and cut into 1-inch pieces

1 lemon, halved

STAPLE INGREDIENT:

Extra-virgin olive oil

1. Whisk ½ cup barbecue sauce, 2 tablespoons olive oil, and 2 tablespoons water together in large bowl. Add tempeh and mushrooms and toss to coat. Thread tempeh onto two 12-inch metal skewers, thread mushrooms onto three 12-inch metal skewers, and thread peppers onto three 12-inch metal skewers.

2. Grill lemon halves over hot fire (covered if using gas), cut sides down, until lightly charred, about 2 minutes; set aside until ready to serve. Add skewered tempeh and vegetables to now-empty grill and grill (covered if using gas), flipping as needed, until tempeh is well browned and vegetables are tender and lightly charred, 10 to 12 minutes.

3. Brush 1 side of skewers with ¼ cup barbecue sauce, flip sauced side down, and grill until sizzling and well browned, about 1 minute. Brush second side with ¼ cup sauce, flip skewers sauced side down, and cook until sizzling and well browned on second side, about 1 minute longer. Transfer to platter and serve with grilled lemons and remaining ¼ cup barbecue sauce.

Round Out Your Meal

Throughout the book, we suggest different optional side dishes to round out your meal, like a grain or simple salad. Here are some ideas to help fill out your plate if you think you need it.

Creamy Parmesan Polenta

SERVES 2 (MAKES ABOUT 2 CUPS)

A pinch of baking soda cuts polenta cooking time in half and eliminates the need for stirring.

2½ cups water
¼ teaspoon table salt
  Pinch baking soda
½ cup coarse-ground cornmeal
1 ounce Parmesan cheese, grated (½ cup)
1 tablespoon unsalted butter

1. Bring water to boil in small saucepan over medium-high heat. Stir in salt and baking soda. Slowly add cornmeal in steady stream, stirring constantly. Bring mixture to boil, stirring constantly, about 30 seconds. Reduce heat to lowest possible setting and cover.

2. After 5 minutes, whisk cornmeal to smooth out any lumps, making sure to scrape down sides and bottom of saucepan. Cover and continue to cook, without stirring, until cornmeal is tender but slightly al dente, 8 to 10 minutes longer. (Polenta should be loose and barely hold its shape; it will continue to thicken as it cools.)

3. Off heat, stir in Parmesan and butter and season with salt and pepper to taste. Cover and let sit for 5 minutes. (Polenta can be refrigerated for up to 3 days.)

Big Batch Creamy Parmesan Polenta
SERVES 4 TO 6 (MAKES ABOUT 6 CUPS)
Increase water to 7½ cups, salt to 1½ teaspoons, cornmeal to 1½ cups, Parmesan to 2 ounces, and butter to 2 tablespoons. Cook the polenta in a large saucepan instead of a small saucepan. Increase the covered cooking time in step 2 to 25 minutes.

Quinoa Pilaf

SERVES 2 (MAKES ABOUT 2 CUPS)

If you buy unwashed quinoa (or if you are unsure whether it's been washed), be sure to rinse it before cooking to remove its bitter protective coating (called saponin).

¾ cup prewashed white quinoa
1¼ cups water or broth
¼ teaspoon table salt

1. Cook quinoa in medium saucepan over medium-high heat, stirring frequently, until very fragrant and making continuous popping sound, 5 to 7 minutes. Stir in water and salt and bring to simmer. Reduce heat to low, cover, and simmer until quinoa is tender and water is absorbed, 18 to 22 minutes, stirring once halfway through cooking.

2. Remove pot from heat and let sit, covered, for 10 minutes, then gently fluff with fork. Season with salt and pepper to taste. (Quinoa can be refrigerated for up to 3 days.)

Big Batch Quinoa Pilaf
SERVES 4 TO 6 (MAKES ABOUT 4 CUPS)
Increase quinoa to 1½ cups, water to 1¾ cups, and salt to ½ teaspoon. Increase covered time in step 2 to 18 to 20 minutes.

Basic Couscous

SERVES 4 TO 6 (MAKES ABOUT 6 CUPS)

- 2 tablespoons unsalted butter
- 2 cups couscous
- 1 cup water
- 1 cup low-sodium chicken broth
- 1 teaspoon table salt

Heat butter in medium saucepan over medium-high heat. When foaming subsides, add couscous and cook, stirring frequently, until grains are just beginning to brown, about 5 minutes. Add water, broth, and salt; stir briefly to combine, cover, and remove pan from heat. Let stand until grains are tender, about 7 minutes. Uncover and fluff grains with fork. Season with pepper to taste and serve. (Couscous can be refrigerated for up to 3 days.)

Short-Grain White Rice

SERVES 4 TO 6 (MAKES ABOUT 4 CUPS)

- 1½ cups short-grain white rice
- 1½ cups water
- ½ teaspoon table salt

Combine all ingredients in medium saucepan and bring to boil over high heat. Reduce heat to low, cover, and simmer for 7 minutes. Let sit off heat for 15 minutes. Serve. (Rice can be refrigerated for up to 3 days.)

Long-Grain White Rice

SERVES 4 TO 6 (MAKES ABOUT 6 CUPS)

2 cups long-grain white rice
3 cups water
½ teaspoon table salt

1. Place rice in fine-mesh strainer and rinse under running water until water running through rice is almost clear, about 1½ minutes, agitating rice with your hand every so often.

2. Combine rice, water, and salt in large saucepan and bring to simmer over high heat. Stir rice with rubber spatula, dislodging any rice that sticks to bottom of saucepan.

3. Cover, reduce heat to low, and cook for 20 minutes. (Steam should steadily emit from sides of saucepan. If water bubbles out from under lid, reduce heat slightly.)

4. Remove from heat; do not uncover. Let stand, covered, for 10 minutes. Gently fluff rice with fork. Serve.

Hands-Off Baked Brown Rice

SERVES 2 (MAKES ABOUT 2 CUPS)

For a basic brown rice recipe that is entirely hands-off, we turn to a loaf pan and the oven. The test kitchen's preferred loaf pan measures 8½ by 4½ inches; if you use a 9 by 5-inch loaf pan, start checking for doneness 5 minutes early.

1¼	cups boiling water or broth
¾	cup long-grain, medium-grain, or short-grain brown rice, rinsed
2	teaspoons extra-virgin olive oil, vegetable oil, or unsalted butter
¼	teaspoon table salt

1. Adjust oven rack to middle position and heat oven to 375 degrees. Combine boiling water, rice, oil, and salt in 8½ by 4½-inch loaf pan. Cover pan tightly with double layer of aluminum foil. Bake until rice is tender and no water remains, 45 to 55 minutes.

2. Remove pan from oven and fluff rice with fork, scraping up any rice that has stuck to bottom. Cover pan with clean dish towel, then re-cover loosely with foil. Let rice sit for 10 minutes. Season with salt and pepper to taste. (Rice can be refrigerated for up to 3 days.)

Big Batch Hands-Off Baked Brown Rice
SERVES 4 TO 6 (MAKES ABOUT 4 CUPS)
Increase boiling water to 2⅓ cups, rice to 1½ cups, and salt to ½ teaspoon. Use an 8-inch square baking dish instead of an 8½ by 4½-inch loaf pan. Increase baking time in step 1 to about 1 hour.

Simple Salad

SERVES 4

This salad makes an elegant pairing with just about any dish. The dressing requires no measuring, no whisking, and (virtually) no thought. (Or, omit the oil and vinegar and try out a Foolproof Vinaigrette, page 252, instead.) For the salad, all you need is lettuce, good quality oil, vinegar, half a garlic clove, salt, and pepper. It's vital to use high-quality ingredients—you can't camouflage wilted lettuce, flavorless oil, or too-harsh vinegar. Try interesting and flavorful leafy greens, such as mesclun, arugula, or Bibb lettuce.

½	garlic clove, peeled
8	ounces (8 cups) lettuce, torn into bite-size pieces if necessary
	Extra-virgin olive oil
	Vinegar

Rub inside of salad bowl with garlic. Add lettuce. Slowly drizzle oil over lettuce, tossing greens very gently, until greens are lightly coated and just glistening. Season with vinegar, salt, and pepper to taste and toss gently to coat. Serve.

Foolproof Vinaigrette

MAKES ABOUT ¼ CUP

This master vinaigrette makes enough to dress 8 cups of greens and works with nearly any type of green. We use two emulsifiers to ensure that the vinaigrette doesn't separate.

- 1 tablespoon red wine, white wine, or champagne vinegar
- 1½ teaspoons very finely minced shallot
- ½ teaspoon regular or light mayonnaise
- ½ teaspoon Dijon mustard
- ⅛ teaspoon table salt
- 3 tablespoons extra-virgin olive oil

1. Whisk vinegar, shallot, mayonnaise, mustard, and salt together in small bowl. Whisk until mixture is milky in appearance and no lumps of mayonnaise remain.

2. Whisking constantly, slowly drizzle in oil until emulsified. If pools of oil gather on surface as you whisk, stop adding oil and whisk mixture well to combine, then resume whisking in oil in slow stream. Vinaigrette should be glossy and lightly thickened, with no pools of oil on surface. Season with pepper to taste.

Foolproof Lemon Vinaigrette
Substitute lemon juice for vinegar. Omit shallot. Add ¼ teaspoon grated lemon zest and pinch sugar along with salt.

Foolproof Balsamic-Mustard Vinaigrette
Substitute balsamic vinegar for wine vinegar, increase mustard to 2 teaspoons, and add ½ teaspoon chopped fresh thyme along with salt.

Foolproof Herb Vinaigrette
Add 1 tablespoon minced fresh parsley or chives and ½ teaspoon minced fresh thyme, tarragon, marjoram, or oregano to vinaigrette just before using.

Skillet Cornbread

SERVES 12

If you don't have buttermilk, you can substitute clabbered milk: Whisk 2 tablespoons lemon juice into 2 cups milk and let the mixture sit until slightly thickened, about 10 minutes. We prefer a cast-iron skillet here, but any ovensafe 10-inch skillet will work fine. Avoid coarsely ground cornmeal as it will make the cornbread gritty.

- 2¼ cups (11¼ ounces) cornmeal
- 2 cups buttermilk
- ¼ cup vegetable oil
- 4 tablespoons unsalted butter, cut into 4 pieces
- 2 large eggs
- 1 teaspoon baking powder
- 1 teaspoon baking soda
- ¾ teaspoon table salt

1. Adjust oven racks to lower-middle and middle positions and heat oven to 450 degrees. Heat 10-inch cast-iron skillet on upper rack for 10 minutes. Spread cornmeal over rimmed baking sheet and bake on lower rack until fragrant and color begins to deepen, about 5 minutes. Transfer hot cornmeal to large bowl and whisk in buttermilk; set aside.

2. Carefully add oil to hot skillet and continue to heat until oil is just smoking, about 5 minutes. Remove skillet from oven and add butter, carefully swirling pan until butter is melted. Pour all but 1 tablespoon oil mixture into cornmeal mixture, leaving remaining oil mixture in pan. Whisk eggs, baking powder, baking soda, and salt into cornmeal mixture.

3. Pour cornmeal mixture into hot skillet and bake until top begins to crack and sides are golden brown, 12 to 16 minutes, rotating pan halfway through baking. Let cornbread cool in pan for 5 minutes, then turn out onto wire rack. Serve.

Perfect Poached Chicken

MAKES 4 CUPS SHREDDED COOKED CHICKEN

We love rotisserie chicken for its convenience and superb shredability. But if you prefer to make your own chicken to shred for tarts, salads, and more, follow this recipe.

    4   (6- to 8-ounce) boneless, skinless
        chicken breasts, trimmed
        Table salt for cooking chicken

1. Cover chicken breasts with plastic wrap and pound thick ends gently until ¾ inch thick. Whisk 4 quarts cool water with 2 tablespoons salt in Dutch oven.

2. Arrange chicken in steamer basket without overlapping. Submerge basket in pot. Heat over medium heat, stirring occasionally, until water registers 175 degrees, 15 to 20 minutes.

3. Turn off heat, cover pot, remove from burner, and let sit until chicken registers 160 degrees, 17 to 22 minutes. Transfer chicken to cutting board and let cool for 10 to 15 minutes. Slice, chop, or shred as desired. Serve. (Chicken can be refrigerated for up to 2 days.)

Nutritional Information for Our Recipes

To calculate the nutritional values of our recipes per serving, we used The Food Processor SQL by ESHA research. When using this program, we entered all the ingredients, using weights wherever possible. We also used our preferred brands in these analyses. Any ingredient listed as "optional" was excluded from the analyses. If there is a range in the serving size, we used the highest number of servings to calculate nutritional values. We did not include additional salt or pepper for food that's seasoned to taste.

	CALORIES	TOTAL FAT (G)	SAT FAT (G)	CHOL (MG)	SODIUM (MG)	TOTAL CARB (G)	DIETARY FIBER (G)	TOTAL SUGARS (G)	PROTEIN (G)
CHICKEN EVERY WAY									
Chicken Noodle Soup	540	27	7	185	580	16	1	2	55
Blue Cheese, Walnut, and Chicken Chopped Salad	560	42	8	100	280	8	4	2	41
Chicken Salad with Whole-Grain Mustard Vinaigrette	320	14	2.5	90	1230	11	1	7	34
Rustic Chicken Tart with Spinach and Brie	550	32	14	115	850	30	2	1	36
Thanksgiving-ish Calzones	870	47	25	160	1450	69	1	18	47
Prosciutto-Wrapped Chicken with Asparagus	560	25	9	220	1240	13	5	6	72
Pan-Seared Chicken with Warm Bulgur Pilaf	580	24	7	190	1010	31	5	3	60
Roasted Chicken with Honey-Glazed Parsnips	750	33	8	175	490	54	11	23	60
Harissa-Rubbed Chicken with Potatoes and Fennel	790	50	10	145	1090	32	5	5	52
Stir-Fried Chicken and Vegetables with Black Bean Garlic Sauce	320	11	1.5	125	560	10	1	3	44
Curried Chicken with Okra	360	16	2	125	1020	13	6	5	41
Cumin-Spiced Chicken Thighs with Cauliflower Couscous	650	46	12	245	1000	14	5	4	46
Chicken Thighs with Fennel, Orange, and Olives	710	52	13	245	790	18	6	10	44
Roasted Chicken and Sweet Potatoes with Garam Masala–Yogurt Sauce	820	52	12	240	990	42	7	14	44

	CALORIES	TOTAL FAT (G)	SAT FAT (G)	CHOL (MG)	SODIUM (MG)	TOTAL CARB (G)	DIETARY FIBER (G)	TOTAL SUGARS (G)	PROTEIN (G)
CHICKEN EVERY WAY (cont.)									
Crispy Chicken with Sautéed Radishes, Spinach, and Bacon	820	57	17	265	990	5	3	1	67
Sheet-Pan Italian Chicken Sausages with Broccoli and Barley	650	35	8	135	1550	46	10	1	41
Lemony Chicken Meatballs with Quinoa and Carrots	720	40	6	100	1080	59	9	9	32
MEATY MEALS									
Almost-Instant Ginger Beef Ramen	410	16	4	75	1900	32	2	3	31
Beef, Tomatillo, and White Bean Stew	400	12	4.5	109	1040	31	8	8	40
Steak with Shichimi Togarashi Charred Cabbage Salad	400	24	8	110	730	12	3	6	37
Steak Tips with Ras El Hanout and Couscous	500	24	7	115	680	29	3	2	40
Rosemary Steak Tips with Gorgonzola Polenta	680	40	19	170	1940	36	5	2	45
Strip Steaks with Cauliflower and Roasted Garlic Butter	670	40	16	165	960	23	8	8	59
Pan-Seared Strip Steaks with Crispy Potatoes	760	46	8	120	880	33	3	2	57
Hearty Potato Leek Soup with Kielbasa	440	20	9	75	1080	52	6	11	16
Smoky Pork and Hominy Soup	320	12	3.5	110	1190	15	2	3	34
Pork Chops with Horseradish Green Beans	490	26	10	180	640	9	3	4	53
Pork Chops with Gochujang Brussels Sprouts	620	37	7	125	860	17	4	6	54
Mustard Pork Chops with Crispy Cabbage	790	40	16	260	1010	9	3	6	89
Roasted Pork with Asparagus, Scallions, and Hoisin-Serrano Butter	490	24	10	180	740	16	3	8	52
Crispy Za'atar Pork with Roasted Acorn Squash	460	16	7	85	860	45	4	8	33
Red Curry–Pork Lettuce Wraps	700	38	14	120	700	52	1	3	34
Polenta with Sausage and Peppers	500	23	11	75	1720	43	6	4	32
Sweet Potato, Celery Root, and Apple Hash with Sausage and Eggs	580	38	15	295	2000	30	4	11	29
'Nduja with Beans and Greens	420	17	5	215	1190	38	12	6	33
Kimchi and Ham Steak Fried Rice	490	12	2.5	50	1940	64	1	5	30

	CALORIES	TOTAL FAT (G)	SAT FAT (G)	CHOL (MG)	SODIUM (MG)	TOTAL CARB (G)	DIETARY FIBER (G)	TOTAL SUGARS (G)	PROTEIN (G)
FRESH CATCH									
Pan-Seared Salmon with Smoked Paprika and Spicy Green Beans	560	35	8	125	880	11	3	4	49
Salmon with Asparagus and Chive Butter Sauce	590	39	12	145	570	5	2	2	49
Roasted Salmon and Broccoli Rabe with Pistachio Gremolata	510	36	7	95	580	6	4	1	40
Salmon and Rice with Cucumber Salad	580	31	6	95	830	37	2	1	41
Lemon-Poached Halibut Packets with Roasted Fingerling Potatoes	350	10	1.5	85	730	29	4	4	35
Sheet-Pan Miso Sea Bass with Kale and Mushrooms	460	25	3.5	85	1010	23	6	8	39
Orange-Tarragon Tilapia with Smoky Green Beans	440	28	12	130	780	11	5	4	39
Lemon-Herb Roasted Cod with Crispy Garlic Potatoes	460	17	7	120	570	32	2	1	44
Sautéed Cod with Roasted Cauliflower and Radishes	380	19	3	75	780	16	6	6	36
Cod with Cilantro Rice	620	36	5	75	680	37	0	0	35
Sesame-Crusted Tuna with Gingery Bok Choy	560	33	1.5	65	1240	9	5	3	51
Seared Scallops with Squash and Sage Butter	220	1	0	40	1260	32	5	5	23
Chipotle Shrimp Risotto	530	23	11	190	760	58	2	2	24
Shrimp with Warm Barley Salad	560	29	8	185	1030	48	9	6	27
Mussels, Chorizo, and Tomatoes with Garlic Toasts	1110	56	16	200	3210	63	4	13	82
NOODLE NIGHT									
Orecchiette with Roasted Garlic, Broccoli Rabe, and Chicken	530	19	3.5	45	520	60	5	2	31
Chicken Lo Mein with Bok Choy	380	15	1.5	110	1310	24	1	22	33
Creamy Egg Noodles with Pork	720	46	20	180	1170	44	0	5	32
Rigatoni with Swiss Chard, Bell Peppers, and Pancetta	470	17	6	35	1060	58	3	3	21
Skillet Tortellini with Sausage and Cherry Tomatoes	560	25	8	85	1540	53	1	5	31
Pasta with 'Nduja Tomato Sauce	380	8	2.5	20	1620	60	4	5	18
Pasta with Sausage Tomato Sauce	370	8	2.5	15	1550	61	4	4	17

	CALORIES	TOTAL FAT (G)	SAT FAT (G)	CHOL (MG)	SODIUM (MG)	TOTAL CARB (G)	DIETARY FIBER (G)	TOTAL SUGARS (G)	PROTEIN (G)
NOODLE NIGHT (cont.)									
Chili-Crisp Steak with Rice Noodles	660	26	6	75	760	80	4	6	30
Lamb Meatballs with Pearl Couscous	780	34	13	85	690	84	2	5	34
Fideos with Shrimp and Fennel	460	16	2.5	215	870	48	4	3	31
Coconut Rice Noodles with Shrimp and Snow Peas	500	23	19	145	310	54	0	2	22
Curried Noodles with Shrimp and Mushrooms	470	20	1.5	145	1030	50	2	2	22
Cauliflower Pasta with Browned Butter–Sage Sauce	510	23	8	30	1110	64	7	5	14
Broccoli-Basil Pasta Salad	600	30	3	0	420	73	6	13	15
Gnocchi with Sun-Dried Tomatoes, Ricotta, and Spinach	490	35	11	110	630	23	1	0	20
Shichimi Togarashi Soba Noodles with Asparagus	460	14	1.5	0	800	70	3	10	17
MEATLESS MONDAYS									
Black Bean Soup	270	3.5	2	5	1430	52	0	4	18
Creamy Chickpea, Broccoli Rabe, and Garlic Soup	260	15	2	0	810	25	8	1	10
Gingery Coconut Carrot Soup with Tofu Croutons	510	43	22	0	540	20	5	7	18
Spiced Red Lentils with Spinach and Crispy Shallots	410	16	1	0	930	51	14	3	19
Warm Broccoli, Chickpea, and Avocado Salad	500	32	4.5	0	1540	48	1	6	15
Farro Salad with Roasted Eggplant	270	9	1	0	460	46	7	8	7
Garlicky Fried Rice with Bok Choy	190	2.5	0	0	500	35	2	2	5
Quinoa with Arugula, Almonds, and Yogurt Sauce	480	27	3.5	5	400	47	6	4	14
Bulgur-Stuffed Acorn Squash with Ras el Hanout	450	23	8	30	740	61	8	15	7
Sautéed Buttery Egg Noodles with Cabbage and Fried Eggs	440	19	8	265	700	50	4	7	17
Lemony Zoodles with Artichokes, Feta, and Pine Nuts	350	26	7	25	1110	20	4	5	11
Broccoli and Goat Cheese Frittata	240	16	6	380	440	4	1	2	18
Curried Roasted Cabbage with Chickpeas	430	22	2	0	1230	46	16	10	14

	CALORIES	TOTAL FAT (G)	SAT FAT (G)	CHOL (MG)	SODIUM (MG)	TOTAL CARB (G)	DIETARY FIBER (G)	TOTAL SUGARS (G)	PROTEIN (G)
MEATLESS MONDAYS (cont.)									
Loaded Sweet Potatoes	310	12	6	30	540	40	8	7	13
Toad-in-a-Hole Sheet-Pan Kimchi Hash Browns	350	14	2.5	185	780	42	0	1	12
Potato and Onion Pizza with Rosemary and Goat Cheese	650	24	7	15	1110	93	6	18	19
Rustic Butternut Squash and Spinach Tart	400	25	9	0	500	48	5	6	6
Cheesy Broccoli Calzones	650	32	18	85	1700	83	2	12	34
Mushroom and Pinto Bean Enchiladas	680	37	11	50	1750	66	6	12	28
Refried Bean and Cheese Melts	440	24	13	60	780	36	1	4	20
DINNER OFF THE GRILL									
Grilled Bread Salad with Chicken and Bell Peppers	640	34	6	175	1010	24	2	7	59
Grilled Chicken, Asparagus, and Endive with Gremolata	370	19	3	125	510	9	5	2	42
Grilled Garam Masala Chicken, Tomatoes, and Naan with Chutney	730	26	4.5	165	1170	60	3	11	62
Grilled Chicken Kebabs with Butternut Squash and Cilantro Vinaigrette	550	34	3.5	135	1030	26	4	5	37
Grilled Steak Tips with Sweet Potatoes, Scallions, and Harissa Sauce	870	57	13	155	1020	37	8	11	51
Grilled Flank Steak with Zucchini and Spicy Honey Butter	480	33	14	145	690	8	2	6	38
Grilled Skirt Steak and Cauliflower with Parsley Vinaigrette	580	42	11	110	920	14	6	5	40
Grilled Strip Steaks with Smashed Cucumber Salad	430	23	11	150	1170	3	2	2	55
Grilled Strip Steaks and Potatoes with Garlic Butter	600	30	12	150	890	28	3	2	55
Grilled Pork Tenderloin Steaks with Grilled Peach and Arugula Salad	390	17	6	120	670	15	2	13	41
Grilled Pork Tenderloin with Broccolini and Hazelnut Browned Butter	640	45	17	205	740	7	5	1	54
Grilled Pork Cutlets and Zucchini with Feta and Mint Compound Butter	290	14	7	120	520	4	1	3	34

	CALORIES	TOTAL FAT (G)	SAT FAT (G)	CHOL (MG)	SODIUM (MG)	TOTAL CARB (G)	DIETARY FIBER (G)	TOTAL SUGARS (G)	PROTEIN (G)
DINNER OFF THE GRILL (cont.)									
Grilled Ribs with Spicy Slaw	1330	88	26	295	4410	52	2	37	80
Grilled Shrimp, Corn, and Avocado Salad	570	40	6	215	1560	30	11	6	30
Grilled Salmon with Charred Red Cabbage Slaw	540	37	7	95	720	16	4	8	37
Grilled Cod and Summer Squash Packets with Crispy Capers	480	30	4.5	100	1060	9	3	5	43
Grilled Swordfish Kebabs with Zucchini Ribbon Salad	670	46	10	165	1300	7	2	4	56
Grilled Vegetable Platter with Pesto	550	38	9	25	1020	40	10	8	15
Grilled Flatbread with Kale and Apples	420	40	14	40	490	11	2	7	4
Grilled Tofu with Charred Broccoli and Peanut Sauce	630	52	5	0	650	19	4	6	25
Grilled Barbecue Tempeh Skewers	430	12	1.5	0	920	62	1	34	18
ROUND OUT YOUR MEAL									
Creamy Parmesan Polenta	200	10	6	25	590	20	2	0	8
Big Batch Creamy Parmesan Polenta	160	7	3.5	15	770	20	2	0	6
Quinoa Pilaf	230	4	0	0	300	41	4	2	9
Big Batch Quinoa Pilaf	230	4	0	0	300	41	4	2	9
Basic Couscous	258	4	3	10	331	45	3	0	8
Short-Grain White Rice	160	1	0	0	200	35	1	0	5
Long-Grain White Rice	234	0	0	0	199	52	0	0	4
Hands-Off Baked Brown Rice	270	8	0.5	0	300	53	5	0	5
Big Batch Hands-Off Baked Brown Rice	250	5	0	0	290	53	5	0	5
Foolproof Vinaigrette (per 2 tablespoons)	100	11	1.5	0	90	0	0	0	0
Foolproof Lemon Vinaigrette (per 2 tablespoons)	100	11	1.5	0	90	0	0	0	0
Foolproof Balsamic-Mustard Vinaigrette (per 2 tablespoons)	110	11	1.5	0	135	1	0	1	0
Foolproof Herb Vinaigrette (per 2 tablespoons)	100	11	1.5	0	90	0	0	0	0
Skillet Cornbread	213	10	3	43	227	25	1	2	5
Perfect Poached Chicken	200	4.5	1	125	220	0	0	0	38

Conversions and Equivalents

Some say cooking is a science and an art. We would say that geography has a hand in it, too. Flours and sugars manufactured in the United Kingdom and elsewhere will feel and taste different from those manufactured in the United States. So we cannot promise that the loaf of bread you bake in Canada or England will taste the same as a loaf baked in the States, but we can offer guidelines for converting weights and measures. We also recommend that you rely on your instincts when making our recipes. Refer to the visual cues provided. If the dough hasn't "come together in a ball" as described, you may need to add more flour—even if the recipe doesn't tell you to. You be the judge.

The recipes in this book were developed using standard U.S. measures following U.S. government guidelines. The charts below offer equivalents for U.S. and metric measures. All conversions are approximate and have been rounded up or down to the nearest whole number.

Example

1 teaspoon = 4.9292 milliliters, rounded up to 5 milliliters
1 ounce = 28.3495 grams, rounded down to 28 grams

VOLUME CONVERSIONS

U.S.	Metric
1 teaspoon	5 milliliters
2 teaspoons	10 milliliters
1 tablespoon	15 milliliters
2 tablespoons	30 milliliters
¼ cup	59 milliliters
⅓ cup	79 milliliters
½ cup	118 milliliters
¾ cup	177 milliliters
1 cup	237 milliliters
1¼ cups	296 milliliters
1½ cups	355 milliliters
2 cups (1 pint)	473 milliliters
2½ cups	591 milliliters
3 cups	710 milliliters
4 cups (1 quart)	0.946 liter
1.06 quarts	1 liter
4 quarts (1 gallon)	3.8 liters

WEIGHT CONVERSIONS

Ounces	Grams
½	14
¾	21
1	28
1½	43
2	57
2½	71
3	85
3½	99
4	113
4½	128
5	142
6	170
7	198
8	227
9	255
10	283
12	340
16 (1 pound)	454

CONVERSIONS FOR COMMON BAKING INGREDIENTS

Baking is an exacting science. Because measuring by weight is far more accurate than measuring by volume, and thus more likely to produce reliable results, in our recipes we provide ounce measures in addition to cup measures for many ingredients. Refer to the chart below to convert these measures into grams.

Ingredient	Ounces	Grams
Flour		
1 cup all-purpose flour*	5	142
1 cup cake flour	4	113
1 cup whole-wheat flour	5½	156
Sugar		
1 cup granulated (white) sugar	7	198
1 cup packed brown sugar (light or dark)	7	198
1 cup confectioners' sugar	4	113
Cocoa Powder		
1 cup cocoa powder	3	85
Butter†		
4 tablespoons (½ stick or ¼ cup)	2	57
8 tablespoons (1 stick or ½ cup)	4	113
16 tablespoons (2 sticks or 1 cup)	8	227

* U.S. all-purpose flour, the most frequently used flour in this book, does not contain leaveners, as some European flours do. These leavened flours are called self-rising or self-raising. If you are using self-rising flour, take this into consideration before adding leaveners to a recipe.

† In the United States, butter is sold both salted and unsalted. We generally recommend unsalted butter. If you are using salted butter, take this into consideration before adding salt to a recipe.

OVEN TEMPERATURES

Fahrenheit	Celsius	Gas Mark
225	105	¼
250	120	½
275	135	1
300	150	2
325	165	3
350	180	4
375	190	5
400	200	6
425	220	7
450	230	8
475	245	9

CONVERTING TEMPERATURES FROM AN INSTANT-READ THERMOMETER

We include doneness temperatures in many of the recipes in this book. We recommend an instant-read thermometer for the job. Refer to the table above to convert Fahrenheit degrees to Celsius. Or, for temperatures not represented in the chart, use this simple formula:

Subtract 32 degrees from the Fahrenheit reading, then divide the result by 1.8 to find the Celsius reading.

Example

"Roast chicken until thighs register 175 degrees."

To convert:

$175°F - 32 = 143°$

$143° \div 1.8 = 79.44°C$, *rounded down to 79°C*

Index

Note: Page references in *italics* indicate photographs.